Religions of the World

This is an inspiring history of faith—the enlightening story of the world's great religions told through the life stories of the world's spiritual leaders.

Here is a complete and colorful explanation of the many faiths by which the world lives and the deities to which it prays.

In this new edition, Mr. Gaer has added interesting statistics on each major religion, including: the number of followers, where they live, founders, sacred books and basic tenets. He has also defined religious beliefs and observances in greater detail, particularly those of the American sects.

"We hope that his book will find its way into the homes of many families, and into the hands of many young people, for it should broaden the minds of all who read it."
—JACKSONVILLE COURIER

"A simply written book, excellent reading for the layman who would like to better understand his neighbors and their beliefs."
—THE CHURCHMAN

D0381463

Other SIGNET and MENTOR Books
of Special Interest

☐ **JEWS, GOD AND HISTORY by Max Dimont.** The 4,000 year history of the Jewish people and their triumphant contributions to the history of Asia, Europe and America. (#Y4172—$1.25)

☐ **THE RELIGIONS OF THE OPPRESSED by Vittorio Lanternari.** A study of modern messianic cults— the fascinating account of the interplay between religion and revolution in the 20th century.
(#MY1047—$1.25)

☐ **WHAT THE GREAT RELIGIONS BELIEVE by Joseph Gaer.** An enlightening account of the world's historic religions with selections from their sacred literature. (#Q4507—95¢)

☐ **VARIETIES OF RELIGIOUS EXPERIENCE by William James.** James' classic work on the psychology of religion and the religious impulse, with an introduction by Jacques Barzun.
(#MY1025—$1.25)

THE NEW AMERICAN LIBRARY, INC.,
P.O. Box 999, Bergenfield, New Jersey 07621

Please send me the SIGNET and MENTOR BOOKS I have checked above. I am enclosing $_____(check or money order—no currency or C.O.D.'s). Please include the list price plus 15¢ a copy to cover handling and mailing costs. (Prices and numbers are subject to change without notice.)

Name_____

Address_____

City_____State_____Zip Code_____
Allow at least 3 weeks for delivery

HOW THE GREAT RELIGIONS BEGAN

JOSEPH GAER

Revised and Enlarged Edition

Ø

A SIGNET BOOK from

NEW AMERICAN LIBRARY

TIMES MIRROR

COPYRIGHT 1929 BY JOSEPH GAER

© 1956 BY JOSEPH GAER

This is an authorized reprint of a hardcover edition published by Dodd, Mead & Company.

SIXTEENTH PRINTING

SIGNET TRADEMARK REG. U.S. PAT. OFF. AND FOREIGN COUNTRIES
REGISTERED TRADEMARK—MARCA REGISTRADA
HECHO EN CHICAGO, U.S.A.

SIGNET, SIGNET CLASSICS, SIGNETTE, MENTOR AND PLUME BOOKS
are published by The New American Library, Inc.,
1301 Avenue of the Americas, New York, New York 10019

PRINTED IN THE UNITED STATES OF AMERICA

TABLE OF CONTENTS

BOOK TWO

RELIGIONS OF CHINA AND JAPAN

Part One: CONFUCIANISM, THE TEACHINGS OF A GREAT SAGE

Part Two: TAOISM, THE RELIGION FEW CAN UNDERSTAND

Part Three: SHINTO, THE WAY OF THE GODS

BOOK THREE

Part One: ZOROASTRIANISM, SPARK OF THE SACRED FIRE

Part Two: JUDAISM, RELIGION OF MANY PROPHETS

Part Three: CHRISTIANITY, STAR OF THE PURPLE EAST

Part Four: MOHAMMEDANISM, FLAMING SWORD OF THE DESERT

PREFACE TO REVISED EDITION

The size of the earth upon which we live has not changed since man first appeared. But in recent years man's means of transportation and communication have changed so radically that the world has suddenly shrunk and the earth has become a very small place. Telegraph poles and telephone wires, radio and television, the train and the automobile, the fast steamship and faster-than-sound airplane —all these have combined to bring distant places near, and to make Ceylon neighbor to Oslo.

Only two or three generations ago we believed that distant peoples were completely different from ourselves; and they believed the same of us. We distrusted them because of their differences; and they distrusted us. They to us, and we to them, were foreign, heathen, strange, and therefore wicked. They were our potential enemies. Our attitudes toward them, and their attitudes toward us, were based on misapprehension, misinformation and misunderstanding.

Now, and suddenly, the North Pole is proximate to the South Pole; and the Equator, only a stone's throw away from any of us. And we must learn not to throw stones, since they may strike the family of the aimer as hard as the aimed-at. We must learn to be good neighbors with all the peoples of the earth as much as with those physically next door to us. Understanding must take the place of misunderstanding. And one basic thing we must try to understand is the faith by which people live; all else is elaboration.

What the faiths of the world are, and how their many forms came to be, is the subject of this book. It attempts to give to the reader a glimpse of how the living religions of the world arose; how they differ; and what they have basically in common one with another.

Since all the living religions were founded centuries ago, nothing basic in them has changed since this book first appeared. But all points that lacked in clarity were rewritten; most names have been transliterated to conform with standard sources; and the salient facts about each religion were placed at the beginning of each section to guide and to orient the reader.

J. G.

Santa Monica, California

1958

HOW THE
GREAT
RELIGIONS
BEGAN

Map of the World
showing the
Distribution Areas
of the
Great Religions

Ocean
FINLAND
Black Sea
Caspian Sea
AFGHANISTAN
IRAN
EGYPT
SAUDI ARABIA
ETHIOPIA
PAKISTAN
UNION OF SOVIET SOCIALIST REPUBLICS
ASIA
MONGOLIA
TIBET
CHINA
INDIA
KOREA
JAPAN
PHILIPPINES
INDO CHINA
Pacific Ocean
Indian Ocean
AUSTRALIA
NEW ZEALAND
Key to Number of Adherents
CHRISTIANITY..
BUDDHISM..
150 TO 520,000,000
MOHAMMEDANISM..
322,000,000
HINDUISM..
310,000,000
CONFUCIANISM..
300 TO 400,000,000
TAOISM..
50,000,000
SHINTO..
30,000,000
JUDAISM..
11,500,000
JAINISM..
1,500,000
ZOROASTRIANISM..
125,000
Note:
The figures on Buddhism, Confucianism, Taoism, and Shinto are approximate since the adherents may also be followers of other religions and may be counted two or three times.

IN THE BEGINNING

As far back in human history as we can go, we find men eager to set the date of the world's creation. The very first account we read in practically every religious literature is a description and an explanation of how the world was created and when man was given dominion over every thing on earth.

According to some of these ancient writings the world we live in was created exactly 4004 years before the Christian Era, or less than six thousand years ago.

Others are not quite so specific, but claim that the world was really created much later than that.

Whereas in India there are people who consider that the world is part of a beginningless and endless process, alternating between the two phases of potentiality and expression—just like the seed and the tree. There is no beginning or ending to the seed and the tree. When at the end of a time cycle, or *kalpa,* the universe is dissolved, it passes into a phase of potentiality, or seed-state, and awaits the next creation. The phase of creation or expression is called "the day of Brahma," and the phase of dissolution or potentiality is called "the night of Brahma." Each day and night of Brahma is a period of exactly 4,320,000,000 human years. The "day of Brahma" we are in at present is called *K'ali yuga,* or the "iron age," and began, according to the folklore of India, 30,101 years before the Christian Era.

Now imagine how old these people think the world is!

But long before people attempted to decipher the blurred date of Creation, they were interested in a great many other questions. In fact, it would seem that primitive man was very queer that way. Like the rest of the creatures of the earth he ate and drank and slept. Like all the rest he wished it were hot when it was cold, and wished it were cold when it was hot. He was also very lazy. But unlike any other creature on earth—he asked questions.

15

Why was among the first words he learned to use, and he used it constantly.

From morning till night he asked questions. Why does the sun shine in the daytime and not at night? Where does the sun go after nightfall? Why does the sickle moon grow fat and round from night to night? Where is the wind when it doesn't blow? Why does it always thunder after lightning? And who made all the things in the world?

These are just a few of the thousands of questions man of long ago asked.

Not only did he ask questions, but he even tried to answer them.

Now asking questions is one thing. Answering them is quite another.

Anyone can ask questions. Anyone can ask: Why is the sky blue? Why has a cat a tail? Why is grass green?

But not everyone can answer these questions correctly.

As an asker of questions the Man of long, long ago was very, very good. But as an answerer of questions he was not so very exact. Like most people to this day, the Man of thousands of years ago used his imagination. If he did not know the answer to any question, he imagined what the answer might be, and then said that *that* was really the answer.

We would say, the Man of long, long ago was a great Story-teller.

"Why does the sun rise each morning and set each night?" the Man of long ago asked.

"That is easy to explain," readily answered his neighbor, the Story-teller. "That sun up there in the skies is a Wheel of Fire on which the Sun-Spirit takes a ride each day across the skies to see the world. At night the Sun-Spirit puts the Wheel of Fire away in the Hall of Darkness and goes to bed. The next morning he takes it out again to take another ride across the skies. But if the Sun-Spirit should feel lazy one day, or angry, he would not take his ride and the sun would not shine, of course."

"If the sun would not shine, how would we be able to go hunting for our food?"

"I don't know!" the Story-teller shrugged his shoulders. "But we can keep the Sun-Spirit from being lazy and angry."

"How?" the Man of long ago asked.

"Easily! When the sun comes up, early in the morning,

we can go up to the mountain-top, so as to be quite close to the sun, then sing to the Sun-Spirit and praise him for not being lazy. That will flatter him and he won't be lazy."

"We'll have to do that," said the Man of long ago, a little sadly.

He did not like the idea of getting up when it was still chilly to climb to the top of a mountain to flatter the Sun-Spirit. But he repeated:

"We'll have to do that!"

And they did.

But if the sun had a Spirit that had to be flattered and praised, surely the moon must also have a Spirit that rode out every night.

As they worshipped the Moon-Spirit, they considered the twinkling stars. The stars, too, were up there in the skies where the Great Spirits lived. They must be the homes of other, if lesser, Spirits. And the Man of long, long ago praised and flattered the stars, too.

Slowly the Spirits to be praised and flattered grew in number.

There was the angry Spirit of the Thunder. And the busy Spirit of the Wind. And the weeping Spirit of the Rain. And the gentle Spirit of the Rivers. And the mysterious Spirit of the Woods. And the restless Spirit of the Ocean. All these, and many, many more the Man of long, long ago praised and worshipped.

The worship of all the Spirits of Nature was the first religion of Mankind. It is called: NATURE WORSHIP.

As time went on, and the people became many on earth, the Spirits they worshipped multiplied rapidly.

"Not only are there Spirits of Nature," said the Story-teller of long, long ago, "but there are other Spirits!" Then he nodded his head knowingly.

"Other Spirits?" people asked, a little frightened.

They really did not like those Spirits very much. They often made them feel uncomfortable. Especially when it was dark.

"Yes," said the Story-teller. "There are other Spirits."

"How do you know?" people asked.

"I remember," the Story-teller began, and looked far away into the woods, "I remember when we were caught in a forest-fire. My mother and I and my two sisters were out picking berries when we were caught by the fire. It was the most terrible fire you can imagine. It came sweeping up the hill, and devoured the forest like a huge bull, with tongues of flame licking up the trees as if they were blades of grass. We looked around and didn't know what to do. Running down would be running into the fire. Running up, the fire travelled faster than the wind and would quickly overtake us. So we just dug a hole very quickly and climbed into that and waited. Later we all came out unhurt, without as much as a scratch or a burn. And who do you think protected us from being burnt by that terrible fire?"

"Who?" the people asked.

"Why, the Spirit of our Family! The Spirit Haba Caba did it!"

"The Spirit of the Sun, we believe, lives on the sun. And the Spirit of the Moon, on the moon. But where does the Spirit of your family live?" the people asked.

"Our Family-Spirit," said the Story-teller, "lives in a frog. Not an ordinary frog, of course. It is a frog the size of that hill yonder. It has only one eye, but its head is covered with ears. And out of its forehead grows a golden horn. We saw it that day we were caught in the forest-fire."

"We never saw such a frog!" The people shook their heads.

"Of course not!" said the Story-teller calmly. "But I'll ask my friend Nandawanda to make an image of our Family-Spirit that you may see him."

Nandawanda made a stone image of a frog as the Story-teller described it, and painted its horn in gold.

"If the Story-teller's family has a Spirit to protect it, surely we must have one, too," people argued.

And they began making images of their Family-Spirits.

Before very long there were thousands and thousands of images. Images made of wood. Images made of clay. Images made of stone. Little images. Big images. Images that looked like wolves, bears, lions, crocodiles, frogs, and fish. Some were half fish and half eagle. Some were half snake and half stag. Some were like cows, ordinary cows. And many looked like no living creature on earth.

The people no longer worshipped the Nature-Spirits, but worshipped these many images, called Idols.

Almost all the people of long ago have in some such way passed from the religion called Nature-Worship, to the worship of images and idols, called: IDOL WORSHIP.

These idols, so the people believed, if flattered enough by prayers and sacrifices, had the power to do good to the people who believed in them, and to harm their enemies.

If a man quarrelled with his neighbor, he would come and pray to his favorite idol to make his neighbor's cow give bloody milk, or in some other way hurt him.

But the neighbors had idols, too. And whilst a man prayed to his own idols to punish and hurt his enemies, his heart was uneasy about what the Spirits of his enemies' idols might do to him and his household.

To protect themselves against the power of the evil spirits that fought on the side of their enemies, people began to wear little images of their idols around their necks. These are called amulets or talismans.

As long as they had those amulets on, so they believed, no evil could befall them.

With certain amulets in their possession they believed they could throw spells on people and perform magic.

Some people began to believe that with certain amulets in their possession and by calling the right names of certain spirits they could open the Gates of the Future and see what was going to happen.

With these beliefs spreading amongst the people, they began spending much of their time in trying to perform magic, and in plotting to harm their enemies through sorcery and witchcraft.

Since every person had some enemies, everybody began to be afraid all the time that their enemies were at that time invoking the evil powers to harm them. If a man became ill, he believed his enemies had wished it upon him through witchcraft, and he started to think of ways to avenge himself.

Some very wise people thought it all over, and realized that at the root of all this evil was Idol-Worship. So they started out to preach against Idol-Worship.

Some of these very wise men who preached against the worship of idols and images established new religions.

The religions they established changed in time as the people in the world changed. Some of the religions that existed in the past no longer exist today, just as some of the nations that existed in the past no longer exist now.

Of the living religions in the world today, some are very old, so old that we really do not know exactly when they began. And some are so young that many people now living can remember when they first started.

There are some people who believe that the word "religion" comes from a word in an ancient language meaning Tree. And religions are, in many ways, like trees.

Like trees, religions begin with a seed. Some do not develop at all. Some die young. And some grow into towering heights with many flourishing branches.

Some religions are already fully grown when others are just beginning to sprout. But all religions are related to each other.

Of the religions followed in the world today, the oldest, as well as one of the greatest and one that has a very large following, is the Religion of the People of India.

And with this religion, and the changes and reforms in this religion, this book

BEGINS:

BOOK ONE

THE RELIGIONS OF INDIA

Part One: BUDDHISM

THE RELIGION OF THE ENLIGHTENED ONE

> This is the True Law of Life,
> said the Buddha:
> *From Good must come Good;
> and from Evil must come Evil*

FOUNDED: 6th Century B. C.

FOUNDER: Siddhartha Gautama, called *The Buddha*
(The Enlightened One), 563-483 B.C.

PLACE: India

SACRED BOOKS: *Tripitaka* (The Three Baskets of Wisdom). The *Tripitaka* are divided into sermons, rules for the priesthood, and elaborations on Buddhist doctrine. Since the *Tripitaka* so many volumes have been added to the Sacred Books of Buddhism that a mere listing of them would take up many pages.

NUMBER OF ADHERENTS: Figures vary from 150,000,-000 to 520,000,000. The difficulty in establishing the number of followers of Buddhism arises because so many are also Confucians and Taoists, and are counted twice or even three times.

DISTRIBUTION: Most Buddhists are in China, Japan, Ceylon, Thailand, Burma, Indo-China, Korea, and Mongolia. There are some Buddhists everywhere in the world. There are extremely few Buddhists in India, the birthplace of Buddhism.

BUDDHISTS IN THE UNITED STATES:
About 165,000

SECTS: Buddhists are divided into followers of: *Hanayana* and *Mahayana,* which might be compared to the Orthodox and Reform branches of other religions. In Tibet it developed into *Lamanism.* In China and Japan, it combined with Confucianism, Taoism and Shinto.

BUDDHISM:
THE RELIGION OF THE ENLIGHTENED ONE

1. A PRINCE IS BORN IN THE LAND OF THE SAKYAS

In the land of India, on the Plains of the Ganges at the foot of the Himalaya Mountains, there lived, about 2500 years ago, a clan of Hindus called the Sakyas, and their ruler King Suddhodhana Gautama.

King Suddhodhana lived in the Royal Palace in Kapila-vista. He was wealthy, and healthy, and all his people loved him. And yet King Suddhodhana was not happy. He had no children.

Each day the King made sacrifices to the many, many gods the Hindus of those days believed in; he gave much in charity; and for many hours studied the Sacred Scriptures of his people. And each day he prayed for a son to rule his people after his death.

When the King was already about fifty years old, Queen Maya gave birth to a son, and he was named Siddhartha, Prince Siddhartha Gautama.

When the news of the Prince's birth became known over the small kingdom of the Sakyas, people from all over the land came to congratulate their King and Queen. On foot, on horseback, and on elephants they came to the Palace bringing with them gifts for their newly-born Prince.

Amongst the many visitors to the Palace came Seven Holy Men from the Himalaya Mountains. When Prince Siddhartha was shown to them, all the Seven Holy Men exclaimed at the same time:

"Such a beautiful child was never born before!"

Then they looked at the little Prince again, and again they exclaimed together:

"He will grow up to be a very great man!"

"What do you foretell for my son?" asked King Suddhodhana very proudly.

"If he chooses a worldly life," the Seven Holy Men replied, "he will become King of the World!"

The great future for his baby-son foretold by such Holy Men made King Suddhodhana very happy. He ordered more sacrifices to be offered up to the gods, more alms to be given to the poor, and the celebration in the Palace to be continued for another seven days.

2. THE QUARREL OF THE COUSINS

When Prince Siddhartha was still very small one of his uncles taught him how to manage elephants. Another uncle taught him how to shoot straight with bow and arrow. And his father taught him how to manage wild horses.

Often the young Prince went out riding through his father's yellow rice-fields, or into the tall forests of mango, tamarind, and sal trees. Or he would run to the banks of the river to watch the snow-capped mountains in the distance grow pink and purple toward evening.

Most of the time he played with his cousins who were about his own age. He had one cousin, called Nanda, with whom he liked to play. He also had a cousin, named Devadattha. But with him he did not like to play because Devadattha was always boasting, and did not always play fair.

Once Prince Siddhartha went into the woods with his cousin Devadattha. Both boys had bows and arrows with them, and Devadattha said:

"Let us see who can shoot straighter, you or I?"

They stuck a white bamboo wand into the ground in front of a dark tree, then walked away twenty paces.

"Now let us see who can split that stick!" said Siddhartha.

"I can!" shouted Devadattha.

"Then you shoot first!"

Devadattha strained his arrow upon his bow and let it fly. It did not hit the mark, but fell close by it.

"I nearly hit it!" Devadattha exclaimed happily.

"Nearly isn't good enough!" Siddhartha repeated what his uncle, who taught him to shoot, often told him.

"Then let me see you do better!" Devadattha challenged.

The young Prince raised his bow, set his arrow taut upon the center of the strained gut, squinted his eyes, then pulled the arrow quickly and let it fly. The arrow hummed through the air and pierced the bamboo wand neatly in the center.

"I can do better than that!" sulked the jealous cousin.

"I can send an arrow that will split your arrow in two!"

He immediately raised his bow and hastily let the arrow fly. Instead of hitting Siddhartha's arrow, it went up into the branches of the tree and struck the wing of a passing pigeon. The bird fell to the ground stunned by the sudden shock. Siddhartha ran to pick it up. He was glad to discover that it was not badly hurt, and he warmed it and calmed it in his hands, then set it free.

"That was my bird!" Devadattha shouted in anger. "You had no right to set it free. It was mine, not yours! It was I who hit it, not you!"

"Yes, you nearly killed it!" answered Siddhartha. "But I saved it. So it was really mine, not yours."

Then they quarrelled long as to whom the bird rightly belonged. Prince Siddhartha insisted that he who kills an innocent creature has no right over it; but he who saves it from death has a right to it.

Devadattha went away very angry. And for many, many years afterwards he remembered this quarrel, and never forgave Prince Siddhartha for having freed the pigeon.

3. THE PRINCE PUTS ON THE SACRED THREAD

When Prince Siddhartha reached his twelfth birthday, a great celebration was arranged in the Royal Palace and many guests were invited. For at that age, as the son of a good Hindu, the Prince had to put on the Sacred Thread, which is a sort of Confirmation.

Before the guests the Prince, like all the boys of his age who put on the Sacred Thread, took the Vow to become an earnest student of the Holy Books of his father's religion.

When a boy puts on the Sacred Thread and takes the Vow of Allegiance to his religion, so the Hindus believe, he becomes born again, and from then on he is called a Twice-Born Hindu.

As soon as Siddhartha became a Twice-Born Hindu, being the King's son, he was sent to the best known and most learned Priests in the Sakya Kingdom to receive from them his education.

In those days children of high Caste studied literature, grammar, mathematics, astronomy and other subjects. But most of their time was devoted to the study of religion.

The books they studied religion from were the *Vedas*,

the Sacred Scriptures of their religion. These were very long books, written mostly in poetry. Besides the *Vedas* they had many other books explaining the Sacred Scriptures. And some of them are very hard to understand.

Before Prince Siddhartha could even begin to study all those books, he had to learn a new language. That was because all the Sacred Books of the Hindus were written not in the language they spoke, but in a very old language called Sanskrit.

As soon as Prince Siddhartha learned to read and understand Sanskrit, his teachers, the Priests, began to teach him the holy books that explained their religion, which is called: HINDUISM.

4. THE RELIGION CALLED HINDUISM

The central creed of Hinduism is that there is one Universal Spirit, without beginning and without end, called *Brahman*, or World-Soul. This World-Soul is also called *Trimutri*, the Three-in-One God. He is called by that name because he is personified in:

1) *Brahma*, the Creator
2) *Vishnu*, the Preserver; and
3) *Shiva*, the Destroyer.

Brahma, so the Hindus believe, created the first Man, named *Manu;* and then he created the first Woman, named Shatarupa. From them have sprung all mankind.

Not all the people in the world were equal, even though they all came from Manu. From the very beginning there were four different kinds of people.

And the four different kinds of people came out of the one Manu in this manner:

Out of Manu's head came the best and holiest people in India, the Priests, called *Brahmins*.

Out of Manu's hands came the next best people, which are the Kings and the Warriors.

Out of Manu's thighs came the craftsmen of the world.

And out of Manu's feet came the rest of the people who belonged to the lowest class.

That was how, so the Priests explained, Brahma, the Creator, made four different kinds of people, some better and some worse. The different kinds of people are called different *Castes*.

The higher the Caste one is born in, the more advantages in life one has. Only members of the highest Caste could be Priests and Teachers of Religion. People born into the lowest Caste could never become Priests, or Rulers, or have important positions of any kind. The higher the Caste one is born into, the more privileges one has. And the lower the Caste one is born into, the fewer advantages one has.

As time went on the Four Castes became divided into many more, until there were thousands of Castes in India.

"If a man of low Caste is very good, and very clever, and very brave, is there no chance for him to enjoy the same advantages in life as of one of the higher Castes?" the people asked.

"No," said the Priests. "If a man is born in one Caste he can never enjoy the advantages of a higher Caste."

"Then there is no use being good," some people decided.

"Yes, there is!" said the Priests. "If you are good in this life, you will be rewarded in the next life."

"Which life?" the people asked.

"As you all know," said the Priests, "every living creature has a soul. This soul comes from the World-Soul, Brahman. Now, Brahman never dies, does he? And so the soul of living things that comes from the World-Soul never dies."

"Then what happens to the soul, when a man dies?"

"When a man dies, his soul comes out of his body and immediately enters into the body of a newly-born babe. If the man leads a good life, he is born again to a higher Caste. If he leads a very bad life, he is born again into a lower Caste."

"What if a man keeps on leading one bad life after another?" some people asked.

"Then he keeps on being born again each time into a lower Caste. He might even be born sick and suffer all his life as a punishment for being bad. Or he might even be born as a dumb animal. A very, very bad man might be born again as an elephant. And if he is a bad elephant, when he dies he might be born again as a dog. And if he is a bad dog, he might go down and down until he is born again as a flea or a mosquito."

(This belief that people's souls enter again into another body after they die, the belief of souls being re-born again and again, is called *Reincarnation*.)

"What makes the souls of good people enter into the bodies of higher Castes, and what makes bad souls enter the bodies of low Castes or animals?" the people wanted to know.

"There is a Law of Life," said the Priests, "that good should be rewarded with good, and evil should be punished with evil. That Law is called KARMA, which means: the Law of the Deed. If one does good, he is rewarded for his good deeds in the next life, and if one does evil, he is punished for it in the next life. That is KARMA."

That was as it should be, the people thought. Good ought to be rewarded, and evil ought to be punished. It seemed right to them that there should be such a law in life as the Law of the Deed, called Karma.

"But what if a man keeps on being good one life after another?"

"Then he is rewarded," the Priests replied. "If a man of a very low Caste leads a good life, then he is born the next time into a higher Caste."

"And if he keeps on being good?" the people asked.

"Then he is born again into a still higher Caste."

"And if he still keeps on being good?"

"Then," said the Priests, "he might go up and up until he becomes a Priest, a Brahmin!"

"And what if the Priest keeps on being good, what is he born into, then?"

"Then," answered the Priests, "then he is not born again any more. Then his Cycle of Lives comes to an end."

"But what happens to that soul that keeps on being good all the time?"

"You remember," said the Priests, "that I told you how all the souls of living things come from Brahman, the World-Soul? Well, when a soul ends the Cycle of Lives it returns to the World-Soul, it becomes one with Brahman. That is called *Nirvana*. And that is the greatest happiness a soul can hope for. Therefore," the Priests added, "you all ought to lead good lives, and do no evil, so that in the end you might hope to become one with the World-Soul and enter *Nirvana*."

These teachings about how the world was created by Brahman, and how mankind came from Manu, the First Man, and about the *Castes,* and *Reincarnation*, and *Karma,* and *Nirvana,* were written down in books. In these books were also written down the names of all the Hindu gods, and all the hymns that ought to be sung to them. Many, many books were written later explaining all these beliefs, and telling the people how they ought to live the good life of the religious Hindu.

When boys, at the age of twelve, became confirmed and put on the Sacred Thread, they began to study all those Sacred Books of their religion.

Prince Siddhartha, too, was taught by the Priests the teachings of their religion, Hinduism.

For four years Prince Siddhartha remained with his teachers, studying. When he returned home to the Royal Palace, at the age of sixteen, he was as learned in the Hindu Religion as any man in the Sakya Kingdom.

5. THE FOUR SIGHTS

On the day Prince Siddhartha was born, on that very day, so one story tells, his future wife, the Princess Yosodhara, was also born.

And now that the Prince was sixteen years old and so very learned, and Princess Yosodhara was sixteen years old and so very beautiful, they were married.

King Suddhodhana gave his son and daughter-in-law three beautiful castles, and many servants, and all that they wished for. And for over ten years Prince Siddhartha and Princess Yosodhara lived very happily together.

The Prince was very fond of hunting, and he often went out on hunting expeditions with his body-guard, Channah.

One day, as the Prince came home from a hunting trip, he saw a man, all skin and bones, writhing in pain upon the ground.

"What is wrong with this man?" the Prince asked Channah.

"This man is ill and in great pain, my Prince!" Channah replied.

"But why is he ill?"

"That, my Prince, is the way of life. All people are liable to become ill."

The Prince asked no more questions. But he became very sad.

The next day, when the Prince and Channah went out again, they met an old man, so old that his back was as curved as a tightened bow. His head nodded all the time. His hands trembled like palm leaves in the breeze. And even with the aid of two canes he could hardly walk.

"What is wrong with this man?" Prince Siddhartha asked Channah. "Is he, too, afflicted with pain and illness?"

"No, my Prince! But he is old, this man, and that is the way of old age."

Again the Prince returned home feeling very sad.

The next day, when Prince Siddhartha and Channah went out again, they met a funeral procession. The corpse of a man was carried to be cremated, and the widow and children of the dead man followed behind, weeping bitterly.

The Prince asked Channah for an explanation.

"This, my Prince, is the way of every man," Channah explained. "No matter whether one is King or Pauper, death comes to all alike."

When the Prince returned home that day, his wife had arranged a great festival in the Entertainment Hall, where many trained girls were to dance and sing and play musical instruments. But the Prince felt too sad to join in the feast. He went away to his room to think over what he had seen.

For nearly thirty years he had lived in palaces, and studied many learned books, but he really knew little of life and people. He had spent many years being amused, hunting, and fishing, and enjoying one festival after another. But now he had seen sickness, and old age, and death. And the longer he thought of these, the more unhappy he became.

Something must be wrong with life, he thought, to have illness and old age and death in it. He wondered where suffering came from. In the many Holy Books he had studied he had not come across an explanation of how suffering was created. He wondered why all the people in his kingdom could not be as happy as he and his family were.

And when he thought of *all* the people in his land, he began to realize how hard and wretched the lives of the very poor people must be. Most of the very poor people belonged to the very low Castes. The poorest were considered so low that they were not even permitted to go into a temple, to read the *Vedas*, or to come near anyone who belonged to the higher Castes. Prince Siddhartha began to realize for the first time in his life how full of suffering the lives of these poor people must be.

He wondered why the Brahma, the Creator, divided

people into so many Castes. That did not seem right. Somehow everything he had learned from the Holy Scriptures and the religious books seemed wrong to him.

As he sat there in his chamber thinking, he heard the sound of music and singing coming from the Entertainment Hall. That made the Prince still more unhappy. For he realized that all pleasures last only for a moment, and all life ends in death. The more he thought about it, and about the suffering that exists in the world, the unhappier he became.

The next day he went out again with Channah. This time he did not go into the woods to hunt, but into the market-place where the people gathered during the day.

There, amongst the merchants, the Prince saw an old monk dressed in coarse yellow robes, begging for food. Though the monk looked old, and was dressed so poorly, and had to beg for his food, his face seemed very calm and happy.

This monk was one of the thousands of people in India who left their families and their homes and went out into the mountains to live by themselves where they could think undisturbed. They only came from time to time to the cities to beg for food.

"If I could live like one of these monks," thought Prince Siddhartha, "and spend all my time thinking, maybe I could learn the truth about where suffering comes from, and how people ought to live in order to lead a good life. Until I discover that truth I will be unhappy."

Then and there the Prince decided to leave the Palace and his family and his wealth, go out into the woods, and live like one of the poor monks.

We have often heard of beggars wanting to become Princes. But here was a Prince in India who decided to become a beggar in order that he might search for the Wisdom of the World.

6. THE GREAT RENUNCIATION

When Prince Siddhartha announced that he was going to leave his home and become a beggar-monk, it was a great shock to his father. King Suddhodhana had hoped that his son would become the next king of the Sakyas, and he tried to persuade the Prince not to leave the Palace. But Siddhartha's mind was made up.

Just at that time Princess Yosodhara gave birth to a boy.

"Now," thought King Suddhodhana, "my son will not leave home. His love for his child will bind him to his home and keep him from becoming a beggar-monk."

But King Suddhodhana was mistaken.

When the child was born, Siddhartha knew that unless he ran away from home before his love for his little son became too great, he would never discover the true Wisdom of Life.

One night he called in Channah and told him to get his favorite horse ready for a long journey.

"Immediately?" asked Channah, surprised that his master should want to start out on a journey after midnight.

"Yes, immediately," Siddhartha replied. "And I want you to come with me. Get ready at once!"

When Channah left to carry out his orders, Prince Siddhartha entered Princess Yosodhara's chamber. There he saw her asleep with her hand resting on the head of the sleeping child beside her. Prince Siddhartha looked lovingly at them, but he did not wake them. He was afraid his heart would weaken at his wife's pleas to remain at home.

He left the Palace with Channah and together they travelled in the direction of the Mogadah Kingdom. When they were a great distance from Kapilavista, they stopped and alighted from their horses. With Channah's help, Siddhartha shaved his head and beard.

On seeing his master shaven like a beggar-monk, Channah began to weep.

"Now, Channah, you return to the Palace, and I will start out on my journey, begging my food, and trying to learn the Truth of Life."

"Yes, my Prince!"

"I am no longer your Prince, Channah! I no longer want to be a ruler over people. I want to be as one of my fellow men that I may understand their lives, and discover how they ought to live in order to lead good happy lives."

"Yes, my Prince!" Channah sobbed.

Channah returned slowly to the Palace in Kapilavista, and Siddhartha started out down the dusty road on foot.

On the way he met a beggar.

"Come," said the Prince to the beggar, "let us change clothes!"

The Prince gave the beggar his beautiful robes, and put on the beggar's clothes in exchange.

Then Prince Siddhartha walked on, a beggar in search of the Wisdom of the World that would explain all of life to him.

That night, when Prince Siddhartha Gautama left his home to become a beggar-monk, in the twenty-ninth year of his life, is known as the *Blessed Night of the Great Renunciation*.

7. THE LONG AND WEARY SEARCH

For seven years Siddhartha wandered from place to place in search of Wisdom. His voice was gentle, his conversation simple and wise. And all the people he met became his friends.

Once, as he sat in a grove of trees talking to some wandering monks, Bimbisara, King of Mogadah, came and listened to him. When Siddhartha ended, King Bimbisara said to him:

"Your words are wise. Come to my Palace and become my Chief Adviser!"

"If it were honor and riches that I sought, I would be King in a Kingdom of the Ganges," Siddhartha replied. "But my search is for things that neither wealth nor honor can buy. For I am in search of the true Knowledge of Life."

"Then," said King Bimbisara, "promise me that when you find that wisdom, you will come and teach it to me!"

"I promise!" said Siddhartha.

Then he left the grove and wandered on, until he reached the great teacher Alara.

"Teach me the Wisdom of the World!" said Siddhartha to Alara.

Alara replied and said:

"Study the Vedas. There you will find the Wisdom of the World!"

Siddhartha wandered on until he came to the great teacher Udaka. And of him, too, he asked:

"Teach me the Wisdom of the World!"

Udaka also answered:

"Study the Vedas, for in them all Wisdom is hidden."

But Siddhartha had spent many years studying the Holy

Scriptures, and in them he had found no explanation why the Brahman made people suffer illness, and old age, and death.

When Siddhartha left the teacher, Udaka, he met five other monks who were also wandering about in search of wisdom.

"In order to gain wisdom, it is written, we must improve our souls," the five monks said. "And to improve our souls we have to torture and starve our bodies. Through great suffering of the body, the soul becomes improved. Such is the teaching of the Brahmins."

"If that is the way to gain wisdom," said Siddhartha, "I shall try that way."

He and the five monks went into a forest together, and there they remained for days. They starved themselves until their bodies became like skeletons, and their feet were too weak to carry them the shortest distance.

One day Siddhartha fainted from hunger, and for a while his friends thought that he was dead. But he recovered. And as soon as he felt strong enough to speak, he said:

"From now on, brethren, I am going to stop starving and torturing myself."

When the other monks heard that, they said to each other:

"Surely Siddhartha is giving up the good life of a truly religious man!"

And they left him.

Siddhartha began to eat and drink, and slowly he regained his strength. The stronger he became the clearer his thoughts became. "The teachings that order men to starve themselves in order to lead the good life, and in that way gain wisdom," thought Siddhartha, "must be wrong. Because the stronger I get the clearer I can think about the world and about religion."

But where suffering came from, and how people ought to live to lead the good life, he still did not know.

Day after day, week after week, and month after month he wandered through the forests and towns, living on berries and fruit he found, and rice given him by the townspeople.

Sometimes he became very tired of this way of living. He longed to see his wife and his little boy. Very often he made up his mind to give up his life as a beggar and return to the Palace. But Siddhartha knew that he would never be happy again in the Palace until he had learned how to end suffering for all mankind.

Once he sat down under a sort of wild fig-tree.

"Here," he said to himself, "I will sit and think of all that I was taught and of all that I have seen in my life. And of these I shall gain wisdom."

For by that time Siddhartha realized that the wisdom and truth he was seeking were not something outside of himself, not some great mystery that was hidden away somewhere at the rainbow's end. He realized that he could not get that wisdom by studying the Vedas, or by starving himself, or by sitting on nails and sharp stones, as some monks did. He now believed that the truth and wisdom a man seeks he can find within himself. All the wisdom and knowledge a man looks for, he thought, are in his own soul and there he ought to search for it.

Then he made a Vow:

"Not until I gain this wisdom will I move from under this tree!"

For hours and hours Siddhartha sat under that tree, comparing the teachings of his religion with all his experiences in life.

Suddenly his face lit up with joy.

"At last," he exclaimed, "I have found the Key to Wisdom! This is the First Law of Life:

"FROM GOOD MUST COME GOOD, AND FROM EVIL MUST COME EVIL."

Siddhartha wondered why he had never thought of that before. For this Law of Life had been known to him all his life. It was one of the important teachings of Brahminism through the Law of the Deed. But now he saw it in a new light. Now he discovered in it the beginning of the wisdom and truth of life that he had been searching for ever since he had left home.

All night long Siddhartha sat there thinking. With the First Law of Life as the Key to Wisdom, he found he could answer all the questions that had troubled him since he became a monk.

The next morning Siddhartha realized that he was at the end of his long search for Wisdom. Now he was the BUDDHA, which means: *The Enlightened One.*

That night, on which Prince Siddhartha Gautama of the Sakya Kingdom became the Buddha (the Enlightened

One), is called by his followers *The Sacred Night*.

And the tree under which he sat during that night is known as the Bo Tree, the *Tree of Wisdom*.

8.   THE SERMON AT BENARES

After the Sacred Night the Buddha remained seven times seven days under the Bo Tree thinking of the First Law of Life, and the wisdom he had gained through that. When all his ideas were so clear to him that he was ready to answer questions about them, he decided to go out and teach them to the world.

First he went to the City of Benares to find the five monks who had deserted him when he began to eat and drink.

"These monks," he thought, "were seeking the truth like myself, and it is easier to teach those who want to learn than those who are not interested."

When he arrived at Benares he found the five monks in a grove of trees outside of the city, sitting close together.

They saw the Buddah coming, and said to each other:

"Here comes Siddhartha who could not lead the life of a good monk. Let us ignore him."

But when he came near, they greeted him and offered him a seat.

"Have you found the wisdom you were seeking?" the monks asked.

"I have," answered the Buddha.

"What *is* the Wisdom of the World?" the monks asked.

"You all believe in *Karma,* in the Law of the Deed, don't you?" the Buddha asked.

"We do!" the five monks answered.

"That is the beginning of Wisdom: *From Good must come Good, and from Evil must come Evil.* That is the First Law of Life, and all things that live are ruled by that Law."

"But that is nothing new," the monks protested.

"But if that Law is true," said the Buddha, "then sacrifices, prayers, and supplications must be foolish."

"Why so?" the monks asked.

"Because," said the Buddha, "water always flows downhill. Fire is always hot. Ice is always cold. Praying to all the gods in India will not make water flow uphill, or fire cold, or ice hot. That is because there are Laws in life that make these things as they are. So also that which is done, cannot be undone again. *Prayers and sacrifices to the gods must therefore be useless."*

"That sounds true," said the monks, agreeing with him.

"If that is true," said the Buddha, "then all the images representing the many gods are useless. If these gods have no power to change anything in the world, they should not be prayed to and worshipped. If a man does good, the results will be good. And if he does evil, the results will be evil, and all the gods in India cannot change that."

"That, too, sounds true," the monks again agreed with him.

"Now, if that is really true," said the Buddha, "it must follow as the day follows night, that the Vedas, which tell people how to pray and how to sacrifice, are not holy. Our priests say to you that the Vedas and every word in them are holy. But I say to you that *the Vedas are not Sacred Books."*

The monks looked at the Buddha in great surprise. No one in India had ever dared to say that the Vedas were not holy.

"Yes," the Buddha added, "the Vedas teach us to believe that Brahma created people in Castes. But that is not true to the First Law of Life. People are only divided into good people and bad people. They who are good, are good; and they who are bad, are bad. And it does not make any difference in what family they are born."

"Then you do not believe Brahma divided the people into Castes?" the monks asked in wonder.

"I do not," the Buddha answered. "I do not believe Brahma created anything. *The world was not created by Brahma."*

"Who then created the world?" the monks asked.

"I believe that the world is going to exist forever and forever. It will never come to an end. And anything that has no end, has no beginning. The world was not created by anyone. *The world always was."*

The monks were silent for a while, thinking of all the Buddha had said which was so different from the teachings they had studied and believed in all their lives.

Suddenly the Buddha addressed the monks and said:

"There are two extremes, O monks, to keep away from. One is a life of pleasure, that is selfish and ignoble. The other is a life of self-torture, and that, too, is unworthy.

For these two roads do not lead to the Good Life."

"Then what is the road one should follow?" the monks asked.

"Follow the Middle-Path!" the Buddha answered.

"How can one find the Middle-Path?"

"By following the Eight-fold Path," the Buddha said.

"And what is the Eight-fold Path?" the monks asked.

The Eight-fold Path teaches the Eight Rules of Life:

Right Belief, which is the belief that Truth is the guide of Man;

Right Resolve, to be calm all the time and never to do harm to any living creature;

Right Speech, never to lie, never to slander anyone, and never to use coarse or harsh language;

Right Behavior, never to steal, never to kill, and never to do anything that one may later regret or be ashamed of;

Right Occupation, never to choose an occupation that is bad, like forgery, the handling of stolen goods, usury, and the like;

Right Effort, always to strive after that which is good, and always to keep away from that which is evil;

Right Contemplation, always to be calm and not allow one's thoughts to be mastered by either joy or sorrow;

Right Concentration is then found when all the other rules have been followed and one has reached the stage of perfect peace.

"This, O monks, is the Eight-fold Path!"

Then he carefully explained again the Eight Rules of Life, and ended by telling them of the Five Commands of Uprightness.

> Do not kill;
> Do not steal;
> Do not lie;
> Do not commit adultery; and
> Do not become intoxicated at any time.

When the Buddha had finished his explanations, the monks said to each other:

"Surely this is wisdom, and surely Siddhartha Gautama has become the Enlightened One: The Buddha. For he has set in motion the wheel of the True Law of Life, the Law that teaches mankind that the world is ruled by Justice."

Then they bowed to the Buddha and told him that they wished to become his followers.

The first sermon that the Buddha preached to the five monks is now famous amongst his followers as The Sermon at Benares.

9. "FROM GOOD MUST COME GOOD."

When the five monks took the Vow to keep the Five Commands of Uprightness, and to believe, as the Buddha believed, that the Vedas were not sacred, and that people are not divided into Castes, but into good people and bad people, then the Buddha organized them into a Brotherhood of Monks.

To these monks he carefully explained all his teachings, and together they started out to spread them throughout the world.

They called these teachings: BUDDHISM.

"I made a promise to King Bimbisara," said the Buddha, "that when I found the wisdom I was seeking I would return and teach it to him. Let us go now to the Mogadah Kingdom, that I may keep my word."

When the king heard that the Buddha was coming, he came out to meet him.

"Have you found the wisdom you were seeking?" the king asked.

"I have, Honored King!"

"And is it hard to understand?"

"The Truth is always simple and easy to understand."

Then the Buddha explained to the king the truths that had come to him under the Bo Tree.

"If I understand you rightly," King Bimbisara said when the Buddha finished, "if I understand you rightly, you do not teach a new religion, but you teach great changes in the old religion, Hinduism."

"It is even as you say," the Buddha replied.

"And from good, you say, must always come good?" King Bimbisara asked.

"That is the Law of Life."

King Bimbisara then became converted to Buddhism, and he helped spread the teaching of Buddhism in his Kingdom.

Before very long the Buddha had many thousands of followers, and his fame travelled from Kingdom to Kingdom, until it reached the Land of the Sakyas.

Once, as the Buddha was preaching to a large number

of his followers, messengers arrived, and said:

"We come from the Land of the Sakyas, and from King Suddhodhana, your father, who implores you to come home and visit him and your family!"

With the King's messengers to lead him, and hundreds of his admirers following him, the Buddha started out for the Palace from which he had run away one dark night, many years before, in search of wisdom.

Upon his arrival home the Buddha preached to his family in the Palace, explaining his teachings.

Prince Rahula, son of the Buddha, approached his father and said:

"Father, I want my inheritance."

The Buddha looked at his disciple, Ananda, who understood his master and gave Prince Rahula the robe of a monk; and the son joined his father's Order.

Now Princess Yosodhara bowed down at the feet of her husband and wanted her share of the treasure that the Buddha had acquired. The Buddha looked at Ananda, who enquired:

"Master, could women be accepted into the Holy Order?"

The Buddha replied:

"Do not the woes of mankind afflict women as well as men?"

Then Princess Yosodhara was made the first nun of the Holy Order of Buddha.

The Buddha's teachings spread through his father's Kingdom, and all the Sakyas accepted them. They called the Buddha *Sakya-muni,* the Wise Man of the Sakyas.

When the Buddha became very famous, his cousin, Devadattha, also joined the Buddha's Order. Devadattha made believe that he was very pious. But he was really jealous of his cousin's fame, and plotted against him. He tried to betray him to the Kings through whose countries the Buddha travelled, but his plans failed, and he was disgraced before the Buddha and his followers.

Wherever the Buddha came, people came in great numbers to hear his sermons.

Once a woman came to the Buddha crying:

"O Enlightened One, my only son has died. I have gone everywhere asking: Is there no way to bring my son back to life again? And they said: Go to the Enlightened

One. He might be able to help you. Can you, O Master, bring my boy back to life again?"

The Buddha looked at her compassionately and said:

"If you bring me some mustard seed from a house in which neither parent, child, relative, nor servant ever died, I shall bring your child back to life again."

The woman went away in search of mustard seed from such a house as the Buddha had described.

For months she went from house to house in her search, and in the end she returned to the Buddha.

"Well, my daughter, have you brought the mustard seed I asked for?"

"No, I have not," she replied. "The people tell me that the living are few, but the dead are many."

The Buddha explained to the weeping mother the truth about suffering, that all of life is suffering, and that the way to the Good Life was through the Eight-fold Path. The woman then joined the Buddhist Sisterhood.

For many years the Buddha and his monks went through the country teaching the Eight-fold Path, helping the poor wherever they could, and gaining many followers.

At the age of eighty the Buddha suddenly became very ill, and he knew that his end was near.

His monks began to weep, and said:

"Our Master is leaving us! Our Master is leaving us!"

The Buddha turned to them and said:

"When I have passed away and am no longer with you, do not think that the Buddha has left you and is not still in your midst. You have my words, my explanations of truth, the laws I have given you. Let them be your guide. The Buddha has not left you."

And after saying this he died.

That was in 483 B.C., over 2400 years ago.

10. THE WISE BIRD AND THE FOOLS

After the Buddha died, his sermons and his sayings were gathered into three collections, called the *Tripitaka,* which means: The Three Baskets of Wisdom. These *Tripitaka* became the Sacred Scriptures of Buddhism.

Besides the Three Baskets of Wisdom, many other books were written about the Buddha, his life and his teachings. One of these books is called the *Jatakas,* which are the stories about the various lives the Buddha lived before he became the Enlightened One.

He lived, according to these stories, about five hundred and thirty lives. Forty-two times he was a god. Eighty-five times he was King. Twenty-four times he was a Prince. Twenty-two times he was a learned man. Twice he was a thief. Once he was a slave. Once he was a gambler. Many times he was a lion, a deer, a horse, an eagle, a bull, a snake, and even a frog. But of course the Bodista (which is the name of the Buddha before he became enlightened) was different from all the other kings and slaves and animals amongst whom he lived. He was always wise.

Here is one story about the Bodista when he was a bird:[1]

"Long ago, when Brahma-datta was reigning in Benares, the Bodista (the name of the Buddha during his former lives before he became enlightened) came to life again as a bird, and lived a forest life, attended by a flock of birds, near a lofty tree, with branches forking out of every side.

"Now one day dust began to fall as the branches of the tree rubbed one against another. The smoke began to rise. The Bodista thought, on seeing this,

'If the two branches go on rubbing like that they will send out sparks of fire and the fire will fall down and seize on the withered leaves; and the tree itself will soon after be consumed. We can't stop here; we ought to get away at once to some other place.' And he addressed the flock in this verse:

> 'The Earth-born tree, on which
> We children of the air depend,
> It, even it, is now emitting fire.
> Seek then the skies, ye birds!
> Behold! our very home and refuge
> Itself has brought forth danger!'

"Then such of the birds as were wise, and hearkened to the voice of the Bodista, flew up at once with him into the air, and went elsewhere. But such as were foolish said one to another, 'Just so! Just so! He's always seeing

[1] *Jataka Tales*, translated by T. W. Rhys Davids from the Pali.

crocodiles in a drop of water!' And paying no attention to what he said, they stopped there.

"And not long afterwards fire was produced precisely in the way the Bodista had foreseen, and the tree caught on fire. And, smoke and flames rising aloft, the birds were blinded by the smoke; they could not get away, and were burned to death!"

All the *Jatakas* tell of the Buddha's life before he became the Enlightened One. After that he was no longer born again. After that he entered *Nirvana*.

11. THE RELIGION FOR ALL MANKIND

When King Bimbisara of Mogadah had heard the Buddha's teachings for the first time, he said:

"If I understand you rightly, you do not teach a new religion, but you teach great changes in the old religion of Hinduism."

"It is even as you say," the Buddha had replied.

But those changes he preached were nevertheless great. So very great were some of the changes he preached that, at least in one way, he did change the old religion completely:

Hinduism was a National Religion. That is to say, it was the religion of only the Hindus and no other people.

All the religions of the world, in the days of the Buddha, were National Religions. Just as all the governments of the world today are National Governments.

The Government of the United States of America makes laws and governs people of the United States of America. But these laws do not govern the people of other countries. The laws made in France are meant for the French people, and not for the German or the Chinese. Each government makes laws for just its own people.

And so it was with all the religions of the world in the days of the Buddha.

Some religions then did not even permit other people to join them. Hinduism was such a religion. It was meant only for those who were *born* Hindus. Anyone who was not born a Hindu, even if he believed everything they believed in and worshipped the gods they worshipped, even then he could not become a follower of Hinduism.

When the Buddha explained that all people could join

his Brotherhood of Monks, no matter what race, color, or nation they belonged to, as long as they were willing to follow the Eight-fold Path, then he started a new kind of religion: A Universal Religion, which means, a religion for all the people in the world.

"In whom there is truth and righteousness he is blessed," said the Buddha. And if that is true for the Hindus, it must also be true for all the people in the world. The Buddha therefore told his monks to go out and teach everybody and everywhere how a man ought to live the good life.

And when the Buddha died his teachings, Buddhism, began to spread to the North and to the South, to the East and to the West, and travelled over all of India, and beyond India. Many, many miles, hundreds of miles, away from India.

12. WHAT HAPPENED TO BUDDHISM

Only about one hundred years after the Buddha's death, his followers began to quarrel amongst themselves as to what their Master meant by many of his teachings, and they gathered in Vesali to discuss their differences.

At that gathering the monks and leaders of Buddhism could not come to any agreement.

Some of the Buddha's teachings lent themselves to different interpretations. His followers were soon divided on the true meaning of the teachings of their Master.

Since they could not come to any agreement, they divided into two groups. As time went on these two groups began to break up into more and more divisions, called Sects.

Many of the Buddhist Priests did not understand what the Buddha taught. And when priests cannot understand the great teachings of their Masters, they try to explain them in their own way. Then they say that their explanations are the only right ones, and all others are wrong. Quite often their explanations teach the very opposite of what their Masters taught.

The Buddha preached against images and image-worship. But his followers set up the Buddha's image in many temples and made the Buddha himself an Idol. And they did many other things that their Master told them not to do.

Slowly the Buddhist religion grew and grew.

About 1200 years after the Buddha's death new religions came into India. Some of these new religions the people liked more than Buddhism. Little by little the teachings of the Buddha lost followers. Until today very few followers of the Buddha are to be found in the Land beyond the Himalayas.

But the teachings of the Buddha travelled East to Nepal, Eastern Turkestan, China and Japan; and South to Burma, Siam, and Ceylon.

Temples have been built all over Asia by the Buddhist followers. In each temple there is a statue of the Buddha. To these images the followers of Buddha bring flowers to place at his feet, and incense to burn before him, to honor his memory. The Buddha is worshipped as though he were a god, and his Three Baskets of Wisdom are the Sacred Scriptures of the Buddhists.

Today, over 2400 years after the death of Prince Siddartha Gautama the Buddha, his teachings still live in the hearts of millions and millions of men and women. And the religion he founded, the first truly Universal Religion in the world, is one of the greatest living religions not only in the number of its followers, but also in the ideals it teaches its followers as to how people ought to live in order to lead the Good Life.

Part Two: JAINISM

THE RELIGION OF MAHAVIRA THE CONQUEROR

> Of Prince Mahavira the Conqueror it is said:
> *He was a great speaker.*
> *He spoke the truth.*

FOUNDED: 6th Century B.C.

FOUNDER: Nataputta Vardhamana, called *Mahavira* (The Great Hero), 599-427 B.C. (Some scholars claim that the dates should be 556-484 B.C.)

PLACE: India

SACRED BOOKS: The *Agamas,* which contain the sermons of the Lord Mahavira. The basic teachings of the *Agamas* are a reverence for life. This religion imposes upon its followers: vegetarianism; opposition to war; asceticism; non-violence even in self-defense.

NUMBER OF ADHERENTS: 1,500,000

DISTRIBUTION: Jains are found almost exclusively in India, and principally in the big cities of central and southern India.

SECTS: The Jains are divided into: *Svetambara* (White-robed), whose priests are always clad in white; and *Digambara* (Sky-clad), whose priests wear nothing but a loincloth. The differences in their clothing are symbolical of their doctrinal differences.

JAINISM:

THE RELIGION OF MAHAVIRA THE CONQUEROR

1. IN THE DAYS OF THE BUDDHA

Prince Gautama the Buddha was not the only one who tried to improve the religion of the Hindus. Even before the Buddha was born there were people in India who were bitterly opposed to the division of people into Castes, and who tried to reform Brahminism.

The most noted of these reformers is known as the Lord Mahavira.

The story of the Lord Mahavira is so much like that of the Buddha that it seems almost the same story, only a little changed.

And that is just what people outside of India thought until about a century ago. But since then a number of scholars have carefully studied many books about the life and teachings of Lord Mahavira, and proven that he was a real person who lived when the Buddha was alive; that he was older than the Buddha; and that he died before the Buddha.

And this is the story of Lord Mahavira:

2. THE BRAVE PRINCE OF VESALI

In the year 600 B.C., over 2500 years ago, the people of the Kingdom of Mogadah, in the north of India, gathered in their Capital, Vesali, for a great celebration.

The streets were lit with many colored lanterns. Sacrifices were offered up at the altars in the temples. Hymns were sung before Brahma, the Creator, and before Vishnu, the Preserver, and before all the other images in the land. And King Sreyama sent out his ministers to distribute alms amongst the poor, and to set all prisoners free.

This was not a religious holiday that the King and his people were celebrating. Nor did they celebrate a great victory over their enemies. For in those days in India the little Kingdoms lived peacefully with their neighbors.

All that festivity was to celebrate the birth of a Prince. The King already had one son to succeed him to the throne after his death. This was his second son, who was named Vardhamana.

Many Holy Men from along the Ganges and the Himalaya Mountains came to see the baby Prince, and foretold a great future for him.

When Prince Vardhamana was still very young one teacher taught him how to use bow and arrow; one teacher taught him how to manage wild horses; and the royal animal-trainer taught him how to manage elephants.

One day Prince Vardhamana was out in the royal gardens playing with the sons of his father's Ministers. What games little boys played in those days I do not know. But whatever games they were, the Prince and his playmates were so engrossed in them that they did not hear the crashing sound coming through the garden until it was almost upon them.

When the sound came quite close and they looked around, they saw an old elephant-bull stampeding directly towards them, madly swinging his powerful trunk.

The boys immediately scattered in all directions, screaming with fear.

All but the Prince.

He stood motionless in the same spot. When the elephant rushed up and was almost upon him, Prince Vardhamana caught hold of its trunk in a way he had been taught by the royal animal-trainer, climbed to the elephant's head, and drove him back to the stables where the keepers soon chained him.

The Prince said nothing to his parents of what had happened. But the animal-trainers came running to the Palace to tell of the Prince's valor. When the incident became known outside the Palace, all the people praised the young Prince for his great courage. The Prince was given a new name, *Mahavira*, which means: Great Hero.

When Prince Mahavira was twelve years old, he put on the Sacred Thread, as was the custom, took the Vow of Allegiance to the religion of his fathers, and was sent to the Priests for several years to study the Hindu Religion.

Prince Mahavira liked to study, but he disliked his teachers. They were all Priests, Brahmins, and thought themselves the best people in the world. Even better than

Kings and Princes. Many of them were very vain. And that the young Prince did not like.

But when Prince Mahavira grew up and was nineteen years old he forgot his hatred of the Priests. For then he became interested in the lovely Princess Yosadha. He married her, and they settled in the Royal Palace with the rest of the Royal Family.

For nearly ten years the Prince and his family lived happily in the Royal Palace of the Kingdom of Mogadah.

But then—

3. THE VOW OF SILENCE

When Prince Mahavira was twenty-eight years old, both his father and mother died, one immediately after the other. They died not through accident or illness, but from slow starvation.

Not that the King and the Queen could not get enough to eat. They starved themselves on purpose.

In those days in India some people considered death by starvation a Holy Death.

King Sreyama and Queen Trisala, who were very religious, starved themselves so that they would die a Holy Death.

The loss of his parents so grieved Prince Mahavira that he went to his older brother, who was now King of Mogadah, and said to him:

"Brother, to mourn the death of our parents I wish to take the Vow that for twelve years I shall neglect my body, and suffer all calamities arising from divine powers, men, or animals."

But his brother, the King, pleaded with him and said:

"Vira, the deaths of our parents are still fresh in our memories. Your leaving us at this time would simply make our sorrows more painful."

Prince Mahavira consented to remain at home for two years. But when the years were over he left home, and went out of the city of Vesali.

At the outskirts of the city he changed his clothes for those of a beggar monk. Then he took another vow, the Vow of Silence:

"From this moment, and for twelve years, I shall not utter a single word!"

After making the Vow of Silence Mahavira started out as a wanderer over the land, as one of the many thousands of monks of India.

When passing through towns and villages, Mahavira would stretch out his cup for kind people to put into it some food. And in the woods he lived upon wild fruit and berries.

Most of the time he spent in the woods or up in the mountains, sitting alone, and thinking about the teachings of his religion.

For twelve years Mahavira went about without once uttering a single word. But if he said nothing in those long years, he thought a great deal. And the longer he thought about his religion, Hinduism, the more he realized that many of its teachings were wrong. Then he thought of ways of changing and improving the teachings of his people's religion.

Once, during his wanderings, Mahavira came to a grazing field outside a village where a shepherd was looking after a small flock of sheep.

"If you will look after my flock whilst I run down to the village for food," said the shepherd to Mahavira, "I'll bring some for you, too."

Mahavira nodded his head in consent, and the shepherd left.

Soon afterwards a wolf came out of the woods, and, before Mahavira could drive him off, he killed a lamb and carried it off. When the shepherd returned and found one of his lambs gone, he demanded an explanation. But Mahavira remained silent.

"What? You will not tell me what became of my lamb, you thief?" the shepherd shouted, and struck Mahavira over the head with his staff.

Mahavira could have explained what became of the lamb, but he did not want to break his Vow of Silence. He was also a much stronger man than the shepherd and could have defended himself, but he had made a vow not to protect himself against any evil that might befall him.

The shepherd kept striking Mahavira until he began to bleed, then he suddenly stopped and looked at the bleeding monk with fear in his eyes.

"You are the first man I ever met," he said in a trembling voice, "who would not protect himself or else run away. You must be a very holy man!"

Mahavira did not answer, but arose and started to walk away.

The shepherd ran after him and asked his forgiveness. Mahavira nodded his head as a sign that he forgave him, and walked on.

The shepherd watched the monk disappear over the hill, and murmured:

"This monk has taught me a great lesson: Silence is stronger than words!"

Mahavira wandered on, thinking:

"This incident has taught me a great lesson: Humility is better than Pride; and Peace is stronger than Anger."

At the end of twelve years, Mahavira did not return home to his family in Vesali, but he went out over the land to spread the ideas that he had patiently thought out during his years of silence.

From place to place he went, preaching to all who would listen to him. Many of his ideas were not new to the people, because they were part of their religion, Hinduism, or other reformers before Mahavira had preached them. But some of Mahavira's ideas were quite new.

"Mahavira is a great speaker," the people said to each other. "He speaks the truth."

Many of them became his followers, and with these he organized a Brotherhood of Monks and a Sisterhood of Nuns.

4. WITHIN YOURSELF LIES SALVATION

Mahavira began his teachings by explaining his belief that all of a man's life was suffering. Birth was suffering; illness was suffering; death was suffering; not getting what one wants is suffering.

"Where does the suffering of the world come from?" some asked Mahavira.

"The suffering of the world comes from Desire," answered Mahavira. "People suffer and are unhappy because they want so many things. No matter how much a man gets of food and wealth and fame, he always wants more. Desire then is the cause of all suffering."

"How are we to do away with suffering?"

"By giving up all desire," Mahavira replied. "When a

man gives up all desire, then he can prepare himself for the greatest happiness of the soul, which is Nirvana."

"What is the way to Nirvana?" people wanted to know.

"The way to Nirvana," Mahavira told them, "is through the *Three Jewels of the Soul*. And these Three Jewels are:

"Right Conviction; Right Knowledge; and *Right Conduct.*

"Right Conduct comes first. And the right conduct of a man is found in the *Five Commandments of the Soul:*

"Do not kill any living thing, or hurt any living thing by word, thought, or deed;

Do not steal;

Do not lie;

Do not live an unchaste life and never become intoxicated;

Do not covet or desire anything.

"Anyone who follows these Commandments leads the Good Life."

Then Mahavira explained that he did not believe in Castes, and that he did not believe prayers have any value or do anyone any good.

"If you do not believe in the holiness of the Castes, and if you do not believe that Brahma created the world, and if you do not believe that making sacrifices to the gods or saying prayers can do a man any good, where then ought one to search for forgiveness from sin that we may enter Nirvana?" people asked Mahavira.

And Mahavira answered:

"Not in prayer, nor in sacrifice, nor in idol-worship will you find forgiveness and the way to the good life. Only by *doing good* can you reach Nirvana. *Within yourselves lies salvation!"*

5. HEAVEN ABOVE AND HELL BELOW

The story of the life of Mahavira seems almost like the story of the life of the Buddha with only a few names and facts changed around.

Both were Hindu Princes; both were very brave boys; both earnestly studied their religion; both were married happily; both left their homes to become beggar monks; both found fault with many of the teachings of their religion; and both came back after years of thinking to preach new teachings to their people.

And the teachings of the two Princes also seem so much alike that, at first, they seem like the teachings of one and the same man.

And yet they established two *very different* religions!

They follow the road of Brahminism as far as *Karma, Reincarnation,* and *Nirvana.*

But when they come to *Holiness of Castes, Salvation by Prayer and Sacrifice,* and the *Absolute Truth of the Vedas* both the Buddha and Mahavira turn away from Brahminism.

They still travel together, both believing that one should not depend upon the help of the gods, but live according to Right Conviction and Right Knowledge.

When Mahavira and the Buddha start out to decide just *what* is the Right Conduct of the Good Man, then Mahavira leaves the Buddha. For here they disagree very much.

The Buddha travels straight ahead on the *Middle Path of Moderation.* He believes that all extremes are evil.

Whereas Mahavira, as you see, turned off on the road of Self-torture, called *Ascetism.* He believes that self-denial and even torture help a man to reach the Good Life.

There are other ways in which these two great teachers differ, but this is the most important difference between them.

Mahavira, like the Buddha, believed that all living things had souls. That they both learned from Brahminism.

But Mahavira also said that even trees and water and fire and certain vegetables have souls. If a man lived a bad life, he might not only be born again in the body of a pig, or a snake, or a frog, but he might even be born again to find himself a carrot, or a beet, or even an onion.

And that was not the worst. Down somewhere, down deep under the surface of the earth, were seven hells, one below the other, and each more terrible. Bad souls that kept on being bad might find themselves in those hells.

Mahavira seemed to believe that souls of living things had weight.

When a soul sins it becomes heavy and sinks down. If it sins very much it might sink down, down, down to the seventh hell.

But when a soul becomes good and pure, it rises and floats up to one of the twenty-six heavens that rise one above the other. When a soul becomes so good and so pure that it is light enough to float up to the twenty-sixth heaven, then it enters Nirvana.

For thirty years Mahavira travelled through India preaching against Castes, and explaining his beliefs in heaven and hell.

When he was seventy years old, he came to a place called Pava. There the Lord Mahavira took ill and could not travel any more. He called together his followers and preached to them his last sermon.

"Of all your teachings, O Master, which is the most important to observe?" one of his followers asked.

"Of all my teachings, the First of my Five Commandments is the most important:

"*Do not kill any living thing, or hurt any living thing by word, thought, or deed.*

"Do not kill animals for food. Do not hunt nor fish, nor ever kill the least creature at any time. Do not kill the mosquito that bites you or the bee that stings you. Do not go to war. Do not fight back your attacker. Do not step upon a worm on the roadside. Even the worm has a soul."

(The First Commandment of Mahavira is known by his followers as *Ahimsa,* which means: Non-injury to anything that has a soul.)

The next morning Mahavira was dead.

The body of Mahavira was cremated in Pava. And to this day the town of Pava, in the Province of Behar, is holy ground for his followers.

6. A RELIGION FOR THE FEW

When Lord Mahavira died there were about 14,000 monks in his Brotherhood. These monks travelled from place to place teaching the words of their Master.

The teachings of Mahavira and all his sermons were gathered into books called AGAMAS, meaning Precepts, and they became the Sacred Scriptures of his followers.

These followers claimed that the Lord Mahavira was not the only founder of their religion. They believed that their religion was founded by twenty-four *Jinas,* twenty-four Conquerors.

And they call their religion, the Religion of the Conquerors, JAINISM.

Their First Conqueror, so they claimed, was the Lord Adinath who appeared on earth many trillions of years ago. And their last Conqueror was the Lord Mahavira.

With these beliefs that their religion was many, many millions and billions and trillions of years old, and with the *Agamas* as their Sacred Scriptures, the Jaina monks started out to preach their religion to the world.

"When the Lord Mahavira preached," the monks said, "not only did all human beings understand him, but even the creatures that crawl, and the birds that fly, and the souls of the vegetables and the trees, all these understood him. And they understood him because he preached a religion for all things that have souls, a religion which is a blessing to all creatures of the world."

But Mahavira's religion could not possibly be a religion for all the people in the world. Because the Jainas are not permitted to till the soil for fear of killing worms. They are not permitted to cut down trees. They are not permitted to do anything that requires the use of furnaces for fear of burning flies and insects. They are not permitted even to boil water for fear of killing insects that are invisible.

If all the people in the world were to become Jainas, then no one could grow fruit and vegetables. No one would be able to make bread to eat. People would not be able to make their clothes, warm their houses, travel anywhere, or do anything. Before very long they would all die of hunger and thirst and cold.

Though in their Sacred Books the Jainas have written down that their religion was meant as "a blessing for all creatures in the world," it was never carried outside of India and never became, nor could become, a Universal Religion.

But in India it soon had many followers, many thousands of followers.

At first the followers of Mahavira did not have any temples, because their teacher did not believe in prayer and in gods. But as time went on they built many temples and put into them stone images of the Lord Mahavira, as well as of the other twenty-three Jinas they believed to have come before Mahavira to bring *Jainism* to the world.

In the beginning these statues were not considered sacred like gods. But in time the people began to worship these statues.

About five hundred years ago a group of monks broke away from the rest of the *Jainas* and formed a new sect that had no images or idols in any of their temples.

There are now about 2,000,000 Jainas in India. They live mostly in Upper Hindustan, along the Ganges River, and in Calcutta.

Because their religion forbids them to be farmers, soldiers, teachers, or manufacturers, they are almost all merchants and bankers. They are very wealthy and the rich Jainas like to spend their money on building temples for their Jinas.

There are about 40,000 of their temples in India today. Some of these are very beautiful. Their temples on Mount Abu are talked of as One of the Seven Wonders of India.

Not only do they build and support temples, but they also keep up old homes for cows and hospitals for sick animals, with wards in them for sick birds and even wards for sick insects.

Queer as their religion may seem to people outside of India, those who have lived amongst the Jainas find them a very kindly people "and better men because of their religion."

Religion to the Jaina is very real and it rules his behavior in everything he does. Every Jaina, even today, has Six Daily Duties to perform. One of these is:

To give charity daily. But the Jaina must never think of it as charity. He must feel it his duty to give to the needy all he can give.

When they go to the temples to pray before the images of their twenty-four Jinas, they ask for the peace and joy of all other living beings before they ask for any favors for themselves. And the favors they usually ask for themselves are not wealth and honor, but the gift of Nirvana.

They often pray in this manner:

> "To the Lord Jinandra, Shri Shanti,
> The worshipped of all the world,
> The Giver of Peace and Joy,
> I bow down my humble head.
> Peace eternal may he award
> To all the beings on earth.
> May I obtain by his favor
> The Highest gift of Nirvana."

Part Three: HINDUSTAN

LAND OF MANY DEITIES

> *Truth is One; sages call It by different names*
>
> Rig Veda

FOUNDED: Prehistoric. It is the oldest of the living religions. According to Hindu tradition, their religion is many thousands of years old.

FOUNDER: There is no individual founder of Hinduism.

PLACE: India

SACRED BOOKS: The *Vedas,* the *Brahmanas* and the *Upanishads.* These are the best known of the Hindu sacred books, but there are many others. The *Bhagavad-Gita,* taken from the epic *Mahabharata,* is best known in the western world, and had, and continues to have, the greatest single influence on adherents of Hinduism.

NUMBER OF ADHERENTS: 310,000,000

DISTRIBUTION: Followers of Hinduism are found principally in India. There are followers also in Ceylon, Bali, Siam, and South Africa.

HINDUS IN THE UNITED STATES: 10,000 in different sects.

SECTS: The sects of Hinduism are numerous and their differences in doctrine and in ritual are very great.

HINDUSTAN:

LAND OF MANY DEITIES

1. THE REFORMERS OF HINDUISM

There were many reformers of Brahminism, as there have been of every old religion.

Some of them succeeded in adding new ideas and beliefs to their religion. A few of them succeeded in changing some of the old beliefs. And there were others, like the Buddha and Mahavira, as we have seen, who established new religions.

Although the Buddha and Mahavira established new religions, they also succeeded in what they originally started out to do, which was to reform and improve Brahminism.

When the Brahmins saw how many people became the followers of the Buddha and the Lord Mahavira, they were afraid that all the people who believed in Brahminism might desert the old religion for the new ones. To keep the Hindus from leaving Hinduism, the Priests accepted some of the teachings from Buddhism and Jainism into the old religion.

All these changes in the religion of India took place amongst themselves, within their own country.

But about eight hundred years ago a great army of Arabs arrived in India, preaching an entirely new religion, called *Mohammedanism*. (Of this religion we shall hear a great deal later in this book.)

These invading Arabs believed that their religion was one for all Mankind, and that all the people in the world ought to accept it.

But these Arabs had a very strange way of persuading people that they ought to join Mohammedanism. Instead of coming to the people with arguments proving that their religion and its teachings were best, they came upon the Hindus with swords. Anyone who did not want to accept Mohammedanism was put to death without mercy.

The Hindus tried to drive the Arabs and their religion out of India.

But they failed. Thousands of Arabs settled in India

and spread their teachings all over the land. After some time their religion had a very large following in India.

The Hindu reformers, who arose from time to time, began to study the religion of the Arabs, and they found in it one belief that they liked very much. That was the belief in One God.

That God was Only One, and not many, and that He ruled the whole world, appealed to the reformers very much. They tried to bring the belief of One God into their old religion.

One such reformer who tried to combine some of the beliefs of Mohammedanism with Brahminism was the great poet Kabir.

2.   THE POET-WEAVER OF BENARES

Nearly five hundred years ago there lived a Brahmin widow in Benares, India, who had a little boy. He was a nice little boy, but she did not know what to do with him. So she placed him in a basket and set him afloat on a lotus pond.

Later in the day a Mohammedan weaver named Niru, and his wife named Nima, came by the pond and saw the basket amongst the flowers, and heard a baby in it cry. Niru, who loved children though he had none of his own, waded out into the water and brought the basket ashore.

When they opened the basket and saw the baby, Nima asked:

"Now what shall we do with him?"

"We'll take him home," said Niru.

"We can't do that," Nima protested. "When we come home the neighbors will come and ask us: 'Who is the mother of a child so beautiful that its eyes are like the lotus?' And what shall we answer them?"

"That's true," said Niru. "But what can we do? If we leave the baby here he will die."

So Nima and her husband took the baby home, named him Kabir, and brought him up as their own child.

As soon as little Kabir was old enough Niru and Nima sent him to the best teachers in Benares. Kabir liked to study, and by the time he was sixteen years old he had learned much of both Mohammedanism and Brahminism. But what interested him most were the teachings of a poet called Ramanand.

Ramanand taught that there is only One God; that Truth is Man's greatest friend; and that living a simple life is the way to Nirvana.

Kabir studied the teachings of Ramanand, and wrote poems about them.

But while he was studying religion, Kabir was also taught by his foster-father to become a weaver.

And when Kabir became a good weaver, he married a girl who had fallen in love with him, and they had two children, one a boy whom they named Kamal, and one a girl whom they named Kamali.

Kabir, we are told, was a very good weaver, a very good student, and a very good father. As he worked at the loom each day, he composed poems into which he put his thoughts about what people ought to believe and do in order to lead the Good Life. These poems became known to all the people of Benares.

Kabir soon became famous as a poet, but he still worked as a simple weaver, earning his livelihood at the loom.

One day Kabir went down to the Ganges River where thousands of Hindus were bathing. The Hindus believe that some of their rivers are sacred and that by bathing in them they can wash away their sins. There are many of these sacred rivers in India, and the most sacred of all is the Ganges.

There Kabir went one day to see the sinners purify themselves.

At the bank of the river Kabir met two Priests. Kabir spoke to them about Ramanand's teachings of the One God.

"We and our forefathers for many, many generations have believed in many gods," the priests said. "So it must be true that there are many gods, not just one."

"As long as the sun does not rise the stars sparkle," Kabir replied.

He was a poet, and often talked in that beautiful way.

"What do you mean by that?" the Priests asked.

"I mean that as long as the perfect knowledge of One God is not known to people, they worship many little gods. But if by worshipping a stone you can find God, I shall worship a mountain. Better than your stone idols are the stones of the flour mill with which men grind their corn."

As they were talking, one of the Priests became thirsty. Kabir dipped his cup into the river and offered the priest a drink. But the priest would not touch it because Kabir was of a lower Caste than himself, and the Brahmins of India believe that one of a higher Caste must not eat or drink from a dish touched by one of a lower Caste.

"If the water of the Ganges cannot purify my cup, how can I believe that it can wash away your sins?" Kabir asked. "The touch of others you Brahmins think makes you unclean. You are puffed up with pride. Great pride never produces any good."

Kabir then left them.

He went back to his work at the loom, to write poetry, and to preach that all men are brothers.

Before very long Kabir had many followers, and his poetry became known far and wide. Still Kabir continued to earn his living as a weaver. He believed that even priests and monks ought to work for their livelihood and not expect people to support them. And he set the example.

In his poetry and sermons he taught against pride and vanity, against the Caste-system of India, and against the worship of idols. And he preached the belief in One God.

When he died in Maghar, at the age of seventy-nine, the Brahmins said that he belonged to them, because he was born a Brahman; and the Mohammedans said that he belonged to them, because he was brought up as a Mohammedan. But when they came and took off the shroud with which his body was covered, so the legend tells, they found a wreath of flowers.

And a wreath of flowers Kabir really left behind him in his teachings, his manner of living, and his poetry.

His followers gathered his sayings and poetry into a book, called the *Bijak,* and they called themselves *Kabir Panthis,* which means: Followers of the Kabir Path.

The *Bijak* is now the Holy Scripture of the *Kabir Panthis.*

There are about a million followers of the Kabir Path in India today, still singing, at their services, the beautiful songs and hymns of Kabir the Weaver.

Kabir's teachings were also studied by later reformers in India who tried to combine them with Brahminism.

One of these was Nanak—Guru Nanak—the Glorious Nanak!

3.   THE RELIGION OF GURU NANAK

In the town of Talwandi, in the Province of Lahore, a son was born to a noble Hindu and his pious wife, and they named him Nanak. That was about four hundred and seventy years ago, when Kabir the Poet-Weaver was nearly thirty years old.

Nanak's father was a poor man, but he tried to give his son a good education. At the age of nine Nanak began to study Persian and Arabic and other languages that were taught in India in those days.

When Nanak grew up he, like Kabir, became interested in Religion. But unlike Kabir, he disliked work of any kind. No matter what his father did, he could not get Nanak to earn his own living.

"If Nanak were married and had a family to support," said his mother, "he would have to work."

"You are right," said his father.

They found a wife for Nanak and he married her. But he still disliked to do any work. Even when his father found a job for him as a government official, Nanak neglected his duties. Instead of going to work each morning, he would go out of town and into the woods, day-dreaming and thinking about the religion of his people. Best of all he liked to spend his days in the woods reading the poetry of Ramanand and Kabir.

When Nanak was thirty years old, he came home one day and announced that he was a *Guru*.

"What is a Guru?" his wife asked.

"A Guru is a teacher of a new religion," Nanak explained.

"And what is this new religion you teach?" his father asked.

"There is no Hindu and no Mohammedan!" Nanak replied.

"How can you say such a thing?" asked Nanak's mother. "There *are* Hindus, and there *are* Mohammedans in our land."

"What I mean," Nanak answered impatiently, "what I mean is that the teachings of the Brahmins are wrong, and the teachings of the Mohammedans are wrong."

"Whose teachings are right?" his father asked.

Nanak then explained his own teachings about the belief in One God, and about there being no Castes, and about it being sinful to worship idols.

"I cannot see in what way your teachings are different from those of Kabir the Poet!" said Nanak's father.

"Kabir teaches that people ought not to eat meat," Nanak explained. "But I teach that people can eat meat, provided the animal to be eaten is killed with one blow of the sword. I also teach that to serve the One True God people must have a leader, a Guru. I am the first Guru of my New Religion, and I shall go out over the land and preach it to the people."

Nanak had a servant called Mordana who could sing very beautifully. And with this servant Nanak started out.

When they came to a market-place or wherever many people passed, Mordana would begin to sing. After he had attracted a crowd, Nanak would get up and preach his religion.

In that way Nanak travelled far over India to Ceylon in the south, and Kashmir in the north, and far into Arabia to the west.

When Nanak died, at the age of seventy, one of his followers called Angad, became the next Guru.

And when Guru Angad died, others followed him as the Teacher of the followers of Nanak.

The fifth Guru, Guru Arjan, collected the sayings of Nanak and his sermons, and the poems of Ramanand and Kabir into a book, called the *Granth Saheb*.

The *Granth Saheb* became the Holy Scriptures of Nanak's followers.

Guru Arjan, the fifth Guru, tried to spread the religion taught by Nanak, called SIKHISM. But the leaders of the other religions did not like the teachings of Sikhism and they objected to Guru Arjan's missionary work.

This angered Guru Arjan very much. He called together all his followers and organized them into an army. Then he went out to spread his religion by the sword, as the Mohammedans did.

When Guru Arjan died, the next leader, Guru Har Govind, became not only the religious leader of the Sikhs, but also the leader of their army. He organized his followers and started a war against the Mohammedan Moghul of India.

One hundred years later the fighting Sikhs established

an independent kingdom, and called themselves an independent nation.

To this day the Sikhs, who number over 3,000,000 members, are still proud of their history as fighters, and most of them are soldiers.

They are easily distinguished from all the other Hindus by what they call the five *Kukkas:*

Kes, which means, long hair;

Kunga, a wooden comb in their hair;

Kach, white drawers worn next to the skin;

Kara, an iron bracelet;

Khanda, a short two-edged dagger that they always wear in the street.

The Sikhs are required to comb their hair at least twice a day. They have to bathe often. And they must read their Holy Scriptures daily.

In Amritsar, which they call their Holy City, they have built a temple, called the *Golden Temple in the Pool of Immortality*. This is one of the most beautiful temples in India, and also one of the most beautiful buildings in the world.

To this temple the Sikhs come to worship their holy *Granth Saheb*. Many of them cannot read, but their Holy Scripture, the book itself, is considered very holy. It is placed on a sort of altar and the Sikhs worship it.

4. HOW A LITTLE MOUSE STARTED A GREAT STIR

After Guru Nanak there were many other reformers in India.

The most important of them was one born only a little over one hundred years ago. He was the son of a very high Caste Hindu, and was called Dayananda.

When Dayananda was old enough, the Sacred Thread was placed upon his neck with great ceremony, and he was sent to the best teachers.

For six years Dayananda remained with his teachers, studying languages and religion. At the end of the six years, when Dayananda returned home, his parents were very proud of their son's great learning.

That year his father wanted Dayananda to keep the Fast of Shivarati.

The Fast of Shivarati is kept by all Hindus who worship the god Shiva. Though all Hindus worship the Three-in-

One God, they also worship each one of the Three separately. Some worship one more than the other. And the third of the Three-in-One God, Shiva, has the greatest number of followers. There are many special holidays and fasts devoted to the god Shiva. And during the Fast of Shivarati people fast a night and a day and another night. The first night of the Fast they sit up all night in the Temple of Shiva singing hymns.

On the eve of the Fast of Shivarati, Dayananda and his father went to the temple, placed rice and flowers upon the idol Shiva, then sat down among the other worshippers to join in the singing of the hymns.

In the beginning they all sang very high and clearly. For hour after hour they sang various hymns from the Vedas.

As the evening passed, and midnight drew near, some of the worshippers began to be tired and sleepy. They lowered their voices. They yawned. They began to blink their heavy eyelids. Their songs sank to a murmur like a breeze passing through low bushes at night.

Dayananda noticed one worshipper's head drop down on his chest as he fell asleep. Another man fell asleep. Then another. As Dayananda looked around he saw many worshippers asleep, his father amongst them. And even the low murmur of the congregation was now almost still.

Dayananda shifted his position, and twisted his head, and moved his hands, and even pinched himself to keep from falling asleep. For he knew that it was supposed to greatly please Shiva to keep awake all through this important night, and he wanted very much to stay awake.

Suddenly he heard a sharp crunching.

Dayananda looked around quickly to where the sound came from, and his eyes grew large with amazement. On the very top of the idol Shiva sat a little mouse crunching the rice that the worshippers had brought to their god.

Dayananda quickly pulled his father's sleeve.

"What is it?" his father asked sleepily.

"Look!" Dayananda whispered and pointed to the mouse.

"What of it?" his father murmured.

"But if Shiva is a god, can't he even drive a mouse away?" Dayananda demanded.

"Ask no questions. An unbeliever asks questions!" his father replied.

But Dayananda was not satisfied with that answer. The little mouse had proven to him that Shiva was just a stone that had no power to do anything.

"I shall not worship idols any more," Dayananda whispered to himself.

He went home, broke the fast, and went to bed.

From that day on Dayananda began to study the various other religions to find out what other people believed in.

His mother said:

"If Dayananda were married and had a family to support he would not have time to study those books of strange religions."

Dayananda's father agreed and chose a bride for his son. But Dayananda did not want to get married. From week to week and from month to month he kept delaying the wedding. Finally his father forced him to set a date, and all the preparations for the wedding were made.

But a few days before the wedding Dayananda disappeared.

5.   THE ASSEMBLY OF THE NOBLE

Dayananda had changed his name, put on the clothes of a beggar, and left his home in search of a teacher who would teach him the truth about religion.

For many years Dayananda wandered through India studying with different learned men. But the teachings of none of them satisfied him. Finally he decided to go to the banks of the Ganges to study from the holy men gathered there.

The Ganges is the most holy river in India. A Hindu with a few drops of Ganges water in his palm would never, never dare swear to a lie. Surely, thought Dayananda, religious teachers there must teach the Truth.

Dayananda went there. Amongst the many religious teachers he found one who hated idols. And with him Dayananda studied.

"You have heard about the *Brahma Samaj*, the Assembly of God, haven't you?" asked this teacher.

"Yes," answered Dayananda. "That is the Assembly of God organized by Rajah Rammohan Roy the very year I was born in."

"Yes, the very year you were born in! Rammohan Roy, like yourself, was not satisfied with all the teachings of Brahminism. He was a great scholar and studied Arabic and Persian and Sanskrit and Hebrew. He made a careful study of a book called the Bible, which is the Sacred Scriptures of Christian Missionaries who have come to our land to spread their religion. In that book he found some teachings he liked very much. And those teachings he tried to combine with the teachings of our religion."

"Then I ought to study the Bible of the Christians," said Dayananda.

For two years he studied the Bible of the Christians and the teachings of Rajah Rammohan Roy. In those two years he became convinced that one ought not to believe in many gods, but in One God; that there are no Castes by birth; but that some people are born more intelligent than others. He also believed, like the Christians, that if a man repents having done anything evil, God forgives his sins. But he still believed in *Reincarnation* and *Nirvana,* as taught by Brahminism, the religion of his country.

After he had all these ideas very clear in his mind, he went out over the land to teach them to others. And he organized his followers into a sect called the *Arya Samaj,* which means:

The Assembly of the Noble.

This sect Dayananda started when he was fifty-one years old, in 1875.

Dayananda died only eight years later. But his work was carried on by his followers. At the present day the Assembly of the Noble is known all over India, and has millions of followers.

6. HINDUISM, AND WHAT IT IS

And so in India and Pakistan today there are many religions and many religious sects.

There are some Jews there and many Christians.

There are about 60,000,000 Mohammedans in that land, mostly in Pakistan.

There are Buddhists; Jainas; Kabir Panthis; Sikhs.

There are the *Brahma Samaj* and the *Arya Samaj.*

There are, in the hill-country, worshippers of trees, rivers, and spirits.

In India, too, lives a little orphan religion that was born in Persia but is now almost entirely in India. (Of this religion, Zoroastrianism, we shall hear later in this book.)

But the greater number of Hindus today, over 300,-000,000 of them, hold fast to various forms of their old religion, Hinduism.

These followers of Hinduism still believe in the Holiness of the Castes. Long, long ago, so they believe, they had only four Castes. But today there are nearly 19,000 different Castes. A man of a higher Caste would not eat or drink together with one of a lower Caste. They would not enter the same Temple. They would not let their children play together. The lower the Caste, the more it is looked down upon. But the Hindu who belongs to even the lowest Caste considers himself superior and better than the millions of people in India, who are called Outcasts.

When an Outcast wants to buy something from the village storekeeper who belongs to a Caste, he does not enter the store. He dares not even come near it. He stands in the street and calls out what he wants and leaves the money in a place specially arranged for that purpose. Then he runs away some distance. The storekeeper brings out what the Outcast wants and takes the money. After the storekeeper returns into the store, the poor Outcast comes and gets the goods the storekeeper left for him in the street.

Hinduism is *the only religion in the world* teaching the belief in the Division of people into Castes.

The followers of Hinduism believe in and worship what appear to be many gods. Their priests tell us that they are not "gods" but representations of different attributes of the ever-present Brahma. There is a representation or image of the quality of "wisdom"; another to represent "learning"; still another to represent "beauty"; and so on. The original thirty-three representations have now multiplied to 33,000,000. And many of the common people, who cannot grasp the abstract idea of an attribute, worship each one as a god.

Today there are so many religious sects, teaching so many differing beliefs, that it is almost impossible to say anything about this religion that would be true for all the sects.

All these various sects of Brahminism are called: HINDUISM.

No matter how different the beliefs of these sects may be, they all lead the same kind of life. *Hinduism is* therefore not so much a religion as *a way of living.*

The followers of the various sects of Hinduism have their own temples. Some dress differently than others. Some have different religious holidays, and they celebrate them differently. But all of them are alike in that they all accept the belief in *Reincarnation* and *Nirvana*.

The most important belief of all these sects of Hinduism is that Man is made up of a Body and a Soul, and that the Soul is the most important part of Man.

How important the Hindus believe the Soul of Man to be is shown in the following story, taken from one of their religious books, called the *Brihad A'ranyaka Upanishad.*

"The Soul is Knowledge!"

There lived a King in Vehedas, 2700 years ago, and his name was Janaka. To this king the great and wise men often came to discuss religion. Amongst them sometimes came the great sage of his time, Yajnavalkya.

Once, when the great Sage was alone with the King, he said to him:

"Great King, I wish to give you a gift to prove my gratitude for your kindness to me. Ask me for whatever is within my means and I shall give it to you."

"If I can choose whatever I please, Great Sage," replied King Janaka, "then permit me to ask you to answer me some questions as your gift to me."

"Ask, Great King, according to your pleasure!" the Sage readily agreed.

"Great Sage, answer me, what light is the Light of Man?" the King asked.

"The light of the sun is the Light of Man, O King! It is by the light of the sun that Man does all his work," the Sage replied.

"It is as you say. But by what light is Man guided when the sun sets?"

"By the light of the moon, Great King! By the light of the moon Man does all his work, after the sun has set."

"But what light is the guide of Man when the moon sets?" the King asked.

"When the moon sets, Man is guided by the light of Fire, O King!"

"It is as you say. But when the fire goes out, what guides Man then?"

"Speech, O King! By speech Man is guided even in the dark."

"But what is the light to guide Man, O Sage, when the sun has set, and the moon has set, and the fire is out, and his speech is silent?"

Then the Sage Yajnavalkya answered and said:

"When the sun has set and the moon has set, and the fire is out, and his speech is silent, then, Great King, the Soul is the Light of Man! For the Soul is Knowledge!"

BOOK TWO

RELIGIONS OF CHINA AND JAPAN

Part One: CONFUCIANISM

The Teachings of a Great Sage

Tzu-kung once asked:

> *"Is there one word that would cover the whole duty of man?"*

To which Confucius replied:

> *"Fellow-feeling, perhaps, is that word. Do not do unto others what thou wouldst not they should do unto you."*

FOUNDED: 6th Century B.C.

FOUNDER: Ch'iu K'ung, later known as *K'ung Fu-tze* (K'ung the Philosopher) and called Confucius, 551-479 B.C. (Exact dates are uncertain.)

PLACE: China

SACRED BOOKS: *Analects* and the *Five K'ing* (or *Ching*) contain the basic teachings of Confucian ethics. Confucius was not a religious teacher, and his teachings were concerned only with the proper way to live. The quintessence of his teachings were: Do not do to others what you do not want them to do to you.

NUMBER OF ADHERENTS: Figures vary from 300,000,-000 to 400,000,000 because Confucians are also Buddhists or Taoists, and it is difficult to estimate their number without duplications.

CONFUCIANS IN THE UNITED STATES: About 165,000

SECTS: There are no sects in Confucianism, for the followers are free to join any other faith. There are millions of Confucians who are also, and at the same time, Buddhists, Taoists, or Christians.

CONFUCIANISM:

The Teachings of a Great Sage

1. HOW THE WORLD WAS CREATED

Long, long ago, long before the world was created, so the Chinese believe, there was Nothing.

NOTHING!

That lasted for a long time. Then Something appeared. And out of Something *P'an Ku* was created.

How long *P'an Ku* lived we are not told. But that he was very big and very strong, that we are told. For when *P'an Ku* died his last groan became the thunder; and his last breath became the wind. His left eye became the sun; and his right eye, the moon. The blood of his veins became the rivers; his hair became the forests, and his flesh became the earth. So big and strong was *P'an Ku*.

And that was how, so the Chinese believe, our world was created.

After that there were people.

Like most people of long ago, the Chinese, of several thousand years ago, were Nature-Worshippers. They believed that the Sun and the Moon and the Wind, the Fire and the Thunder and the Lightning, and the Mountains and the Rivers all had spirits that should be worshipped.

Over these spirits, as well as over all the people, there was One Supreme Ruler, called *Shang Ti. Shang Ti* was very just. So just was he that no matter how much the wicked prayed to him, he would do nothing for them.

But *Shang Ti* was not the highest god. The highest and greatest god, so the Chinese believed, was the God of Gods, called *T'ien,* and he lived in Heaven.

The way the Chinese found out where T'ien, God of Gods, lived was really very simple:

The rain they needed so badly for their rice-fields came from the sky above.

The clouds that carried the rain they needed so badly for their rice-fields were also above in the sky.

The wind that brought the clouds that carried the rain

they needed so badly for their rice-fields came also from the sky above.

The thunder and lightning that opened the clouds the wind had brought and that poured down the rain they needed so badly for their rice-fields were also above in the sky.

And even the rainbow after the rain that all could see but no one could touch, that, too, was in the sky.

Then surely T'ien, the God of Gods, must live above in Heaven!

And so the Chinese of long ago worshipped the God of Gods, and the Supreme Ruler who was so very Just, and the Spirits of the Sun, the Moon, the Rain, Fire, Thunder, the Mountains, and the Rivers.

They also worshipped the spirits of their ancestors.

When a man died his sons worshipped his spirit. His grandsons, too, worshipped him. And even his great-grandsons, and his great-great-grandsons worshipped his memory. Not only did people worship the spirits of their parents, grandparents, and great-grandparents, but they also worshipped the spirits of all the great sages, and National Heroes of China. They especially worshipped their Emperors, who were considered very holy.

This worship of the spirits of their ancestors is called ANCESTOR-WORSHIP.

Nearly five thousand years ago the Yellow Emperor of the Flowery Kingdom built the first temple to the spirit of the Mountains and the Rivers. After that many other temples were built in China to many other spirits. Later one Emperor told his people to have music in the temples because, he said, the gods must love music.

And so for many, many years the people of the Flowery Kingdom worshipped their ancestors, sang songs and played lutes in their temples, and offered up sacrifices to all the spirits of nature.

2. SHUH-LIANG HEIH THE VALIANT

In the Province of Lu, in the District of Tsow, not far from the River Hwang-ho in China, there lived, over 2500 years ago, a man named Shuh-liang Heih, whose family name was K'ung.

Shuh-liang Heih was a big man, over seven feet in

height, and broad across the shoulders like a quiet river. About his strength and about his valor many stories were told amongst his people. And these stories travelled from district to district until they were known all over Lu. And even in Ch'i, and even in Ts'in the valor of Shuh-liang Heih was known and admired.

Shuh-liang Heih was of royal descent, and he was in command over the district of Tsow near the Yellow River, not far from the Yellow Sea.

Once, it is told, Shuh-liang Heih was leading an army and besieged the fortress of an enemy of Tsow. The entrance of the fortress was left open, and many of Heih's men rushed into it. When they were inside, the enemy at once began to lower the gates to trap the soldiers of Tsow. Just then Shuh-liang Heih the Valiant rushed up to the immense gates, raised them with his hands, and held them there until all his men passed through and escaped.

Such a strong man was greatly admired in those days in China. For the Chinese Empire was then divided into little states, each ruled by a Duke or a Prince, and each one looking out for his own interests. Those were bad days in China, and a strong and valiant man who could help his Prince was much sought after and admired.

Shuh-liang Heih ought to have been a very happy man. But he was not. Heih the Valiant was married and had nine children, but they were all girls. And in China girls counted for little. Because girls grew up and got married. And then, according to custom, they worshipped the spirits of their husbands' ancestors. And Heih, like the rest of his people, wanted a son to worship his spirit after his death. So Shuh-liang Heih was not happy.

But when he was seventy years old his wife, Ching-Tsai, gave birth to a son. And they named him Ch'iu.

That was in 551 B.C., or 2480 years ago.

When young Ch'iu was only three years old, his father, Shuh-liang Heih, died.

And so little Ch'iu K'ung was left fatherless at the age of three, in the District of Tsow, in the Province of Lu, which is now Shantung by the Yellow Sea.

3.   WHEN CH'IU K'UNG WAS STILL YOUNG

Though Shuh-liang Heih was Governor of Tsow before he died, he left his wife very poor. Yet she managed to give her only son a good education. And she was very happy when little Ch'iu was praised by his teachers for his interest in studies and his understanding of things that even grown people had difficulty in understanding.

As Ch'iu K'ung grew up, his great learning and wisdom became known all over the district he lived in. And many people came to talk with him and to listen to what he had to say.

When he was nineteen years old he married and set up a home of his own. It was then, too, that he was given the position of Keeper of Granaries.

Though he was still so very young when he became Keeper of Granaries, he made so many improvements, that the Minister of Tsow promoted him to the position of Superintendent of Fields of their District.

That was a very important position for a young man only twenty years old, yet K'ung wished he could give it all up to devote himself to the study of poetry and music. But his wife gave birth to a boy, and he had to keep his position to support his family.

Though his daily duties as Superintendent of Fields kept K'ung very busy, he spent many hours of his leisure studying history, music, and poetry. His knowledge increased daily. And the reputation of his learning was carried over the length and breadth of Tsow.

His home became the meeting place of all the learned men of his District. Almost every evening men of all ages came to K'ung to ask him questions and to be taught how to know what was right and what was wrong. And young Ch'iu was always glad to teach whatever he knew to those who were willing to learn.

Many of the people who came to the house of the young Superintendent of Fields called him *K'ung-fu-tze*, which means: K'ung the Philosopher. We pronounce it *Confucius*.

All went well with the wise Confucius until he was twenty-three years old. But at that time Ching-Tsai, his mother, died.

4. THE GROWING FAME OF A GREAT TEACHER

When his mother died, Confucius resigned from his position as Superintendent of Fields to mourn her death for three years.

Such was, and still is, the custom in China: when either a father or a mother dies, the son goes into mourning for twenty-seven months, or for three years.

The three years of mourning Confucius devoted to the study of the history of his people and their poetry and philosophy.

When the days of his mourning were over, Confucius did not return to his government position, but went on with his studies. And to earn a livelihood for himself and his family he began to teach.

His fame as a teacher became so great that students flocked to him from all over the Province of Lu, and from Provinces beyond Lu. The number of his students grew from day to day. When he was thirty-four years old Confucius had over 3,000 pupils and followers.

Just then the Chief Minister of the Province of Lu became very ill, and knew that he would soon die. He called his only son to his bedside and said to him:

"My son, in my young days I studied little, and all my life I was sorry for it. I want you to study hard and become well educated."

"Yes, father!" his son replied.

"I have heard of Confucius whose wisdom has no equal in our land. Go to him, my son, and study with him!"

"I will!" the son promised.

When the Chief Minister of Lu died, his son kept his promise to his father and went to study with Confucius. Through the son of the Chief Minister, the Duke of Lu became a friend of Confucius, and that helped spread the fame of the young philosopher.

Once a civil war broke out in the Province of Lu, and the Duke had to run away from home for his life. Confucius, who was a close friend of the Duke, also ran away to the neighboring Province of Ts'i. But Confucius did not like to live away from home. As soon as the war was over, he returned to Lu and continued teaching and studying.

By this time Confucius' son, Le, had grown up, but he proved a disappointment to his famous father.

Once we are told, Le came across his father in a hall where Confucius was alone.

"Le, do you study poetry?" Confucius asked him.

"No," Le replied shamefacedly.

"He who does not study poetry," his father said sternly,

"is like a man with his face turned to the wall. Does a man with his face turned to the wall ever see anything beautiful?"

Confucius then turned away from his son, greatly grieved.

But if Confucius was disappointed in his own son, he had several young pupils whom he loved dearly, and for whom he predicted great futures. These pupils he taught, and with these he studied untiringly.

5. WHEN THE PRISONS WERE EMPTY IN LU

When Confucius was fifty-two years old, the people of the town of Chung-tu came to him and said:

"We have heard of your great wisdom, Confucius, and we want you to come and be the Chief-Magistrate in our town."

Being Chief-Magistrate was something like being a Mayor.

After Confucius thought it over, he accepted their offer and became the Chief-Magistrate of Chung-tu.

Before a year was over the town Chung-tu became famous all over the Province of Lu.

"Since Confucius became its Chief-Magistrate," it was said, "it would be hard to find people happier and more loyal than the people of Chung-tu."

When the Duke of Lu heard about it, he sent for Confucius.

"Confucius," said the Duke, "I have been told that since you became Chief-Magistrate of Chung-tu, you have made many changes in the city government."

"You have been correctly informed, Honored Duke!" Confucius replied.

"I have been told that since you have been in office the people of your city have been happy and most loyal. How did you manage to do it in so short a time?"

"I rewarded those who were good, and I punished those who were bad. The people saw that it was good to be good and bad to be bad, and they became good. And good people are loyal to each other and to the government."

"But how did you manage to make them happy?"

"I chose wise people to teach them and to take care of

them as if they were their children. Though people cannot always be made to understand, they can always be made to follow. And when they follow the good and wise, they are happy."

"Can one rule an entire Province the same way as you rule your city?" the Duke asked.

"Even an Empire, Honored Duke!" Confucius replied.

When the Duke heard that, he asked Confucius to become Minister of Crime for the entire Province of Lu.

As soon as Confucius became Minister of Crime he began to study the prisons in the Province of Lu, and the kind of people that filled them all over the land.

After a long time of studying and investigating, Confucius called together the judges, and the lawyers, and the wardens who worked under him, and said to them:

"I have made a study of our prisons, and I have discovered that almost all of the prisoners are poor people, or children of the poor. I also discovered that almost all the prisoners are ignorant, or the children of the ignorant. It seems to me then that poverty and ignorance make people commit crimes and break our laws. If we could do away with poverty and ignorance then we would have no more crime in our land."

"But how are we to do away with poverty and ignorance?" one of the Judges asked.

"The way to do away with ignorance," Confucius replied, "is through education. If we educate all the people in our Province, then we will do away with ignorance. And we can do away with poverty by teaching the people useful trades and occupations so that they can always earn an honest living."

"How shall we begin to make these changes?" another of the Judges asked.

"You are their rulers," Confucius replied. "It is your duty to be good. People need rulers whom they can follow. If the rulers are corrupt, the people also will be corrupt. But if the rulers are good, the people will follow their example and also be good. And the first rule for being good is: Do not do anything to others that you would not want them to do to you."

After two years of Confucius' rule as Minister of Crime, all the prisons and the courts of the Province of Lu were empty and deserted.

The Judges had nothing to do.

The Lawyers had nothing to do.

And the wardens of the prisons had nothing to do.

For there were no longer any criminals in Lu.

At that time the new Duke of Lu was a young man named Ting. Ting saw what a wise man Confucius was, and he began to consult him on all matters of government, and to follow the philosopher's advice.

The Province of Lu soon became rich and powerful.

That, of course, made the Dukes and Ministers of the other Provinces in China very jealous. So they said to each other:

"With Confucius at the head of its government, Lu will soon become the richest and strongest Province in the entire Empire. What can we do to stop it?"

One Minister said:

"If we could only keep the young Duke Ting from listening to the advice of Confucius, his Province would soon become as poor and as bad as it was before."

"But how are we to stop Ting from listening to Confucius?" another Minister wanted to know.

They thought, and thought, and thought, and finally decided to send Duke Ting gifts of dancing girls and race-horses.

After Duke Ting received these gifts he spent all his time on the race-tracks. Confucius realized that the government was neglected. But each time he came to the Palace to remind the Duke of things that ought to be done, the Duke was away, or he would not want to see him.

In a short time the prosperous Lu became poor, and the prisons filled with criminals.

Confucius, who was greatly grieved to see all his good work undone, decided to leave his native Province.

"If I could get a ruler who would listen to me for one year," he said to his followers, "my dream of a state where all the people are good and happy would soon come true!"

6. THE MASTER AND THE HERMIT

With a number of his followers Confucius started out in search of a just ruler who wished to learn how to make his people good and happy.

On their travels Confucius and his followers once came to a river they wanted to cross. But it had no bridge.

"Tzu-lu," said Confucius to one of his followers, "go over to that man working in the field and ask him where we can get a ferry to cross this river. He may know."

When Tzu-lu came near the man, he saw that it was Chang-chu, a hermit. There were many hermits in China then. Many people were infuriated by the selfishness of the Duke and the Ministers, and left the towns and villages to go and live all by themselves. Chang-chu was one such hermit.

When Tzu-lu came near, Chang-chu asked him:

"Who are you, sir?"

"I am Tzu-lu."

"Are you the follower of K'ung-fu-tze?"

"The same," Tzu-lu replied.

"Would it not be better if you were to become a hermit, rather than follow a master who runs around from one Province to another?"

Then the hermit went on with his work in the field and would not tell Tzu-lu where they could get a ferry to cross the river.

Tzu-lu returned to Confucius and told him what Chang-chu had said.

"Chang-chu is wrong," said Confucius. "By running away from evil one does not change it for the better. If all the people were good and happy there would be no need for me to try to set them straight. It is the duty of every man not to run away when there is trouble. *To see what is right and not to do it, that is cowardice.*"

The followers of Confucius realized how much wiser was their Master's way than that of the hermit.

Later that day Confucius said to his followers:

"Good is no hermit. It has many neighbors."

And they all smiled.

7. A HEART SET ON LOVE CAN DO NO WRONG

For fifteen years Confucius and his followers wandered in search of a wise ruler, and found none. While he was away in foreign Provinces, Confucius' wife died. And by the time he returned to Lu he was already growing old.

The Duke of Lu asked Confucius to become his Chief

Adviser. But Confucius decided to spend the remainder of his life in writing a history of Lu, and in gathering a collection of Old Chinese poetry.

Through his books Confucius hoped that his ideas would be carried all over China. And his pupils and followers, he hoped, would help spread his teachings. Amongst his followers were a number of famous scholars, and with them he spent many hours in discussion.

What Confucius particularly liked to discuss was the importance of Education. Knowledge, he believed, was the greatest good in the world.

"Is education good for all people?" one of his followers once asked him.

"A man who studied for three years and did not derive any good from it would be hard to find," Confucius replied.

"And is it good to study at all times?" another follower asked.

"It is good to study at all times, but it is better if people become educated when they are still young."

"Would it be right if a man were liked by all his neighbors?" one of his students wanted to know.

"No," said Confucius.

"Then would it be right if a man were hated by all his neighbors?"

"No," said Confucius. "It would be better if the good men in the neighborhood liked him and the bad men in the neighborhood hated him."

"Would it be right to repay good for evil?" another student wanted to know.

"No," Confucius replied. "For how then would you repay good? Repay good with good, and evil with justice."

Confucius was always ready to answer questions about how people ought to live, what they are to learn, and how one can become a Good Man. But he refused to answer questions about any god, or heaven, or life after death.

When asked whether he thought that there was a life after death, he replied:

"Not knowing about life, how can we know about death?"

And he would say no more.

But just as there were some things he would not talk about, there were many things he particularly loved to discuss. He enjoyed talking about the ways of the Good Man, about poetry and music, and, above all, he loved to talk about love.

"What is love?" one of his followers asked him.

"To love mankind, that is love," he replied.

"But what is it?"

To hold dear the effort more than the prize may be called love. The joy of doing something not for the prize one would get in the end, but for the joy itself, that may be called love. To do good not because you are going to be rewarded for it in this life or in a life to come, but to do good because you enjoy doing good, that is to love good. Love is its own reward. Love makes all things look beautiful. Love offers peace. When love is at stake, my children, yield not to an army!"

He thought for a while, then added:

"A heart set on love can do no wrong!"

8. THE LAST DAYS OF THE GREAT SAGE

Confucius was growing old. Although he worked hard on the books he was gathering and writing, the thought of the poverty and misery all over China saddened him.

Then one of his beloved pupils died. And when Confucius reached his seventieth birthday his son, Le, died.

But Le left a son behind him, named Keigh, who was very much like his grandfather, Confucius. Keigh lived with his grandfather, studied with him, and was a great joy to the old philosopher.

Confucius was alone in his room one day, working on his book of history which he called *Autumn and Spring,* when Keigh came into the room quietly so as not to disturb his grandfather. Confucius worked on for some time, then he stopped writing and sighed.

"Grandpa," Keigh asked softly, "Grandpa, why do you sigh? Is it because you think your descendants will be unworthy of you? Or is it that in your admiration of the great sages who came before you, you fear that you fall short of them?"

Confucius rose from his seat and came over to his grandson.

"Child," he asked as he put his hand on the boy's shoulder, "how is it that you know my thoughts?"

"Well, I have often heard you say that when the father has gathered and prepared the wood, if the son cannot carry the bundle he is to be called unworthy. This thought often comes to my mind and it fills me with fear that I may be unworthy to carry on your work."

Confucius was delighted with his grandson's reply. He smiled happily, and exclaimed:

"Now shall I be without worry! My teachings will not be wasted. They will be carried on and flourish!"

Then he seated himself again, and said:

"Come, child, sit down beside me."

And when Keigh sat down near him, Confucius said:

"There are men in every town who have as much understanding as I have. But when I am asked about something I try to sift it to the bottom until I understand it. There are many men as wise as I am, but few who are as fond of learning."

"When can it be said of a man that he has learning?" Keigh asked.

"When can it be said of a man that he is good in archery?" Confucius answered the question with a question, as he often did.

"When he can hit the mark," Keigh replied.

"That also is true of learning," said Confucius. "To pierce through the target does not score in archery. It is hitting the mark that counts. It is the man who hits the mark of good behavior and understanding who might be said to have learning. And he who has learning keeps away from extremes of any kind. Not going far enough is bad, and going too far is not any better. The man who knows how to keep to the middle between extremes has understanding."

"And how is one to know whether he is going far enough, yet not too far? How is one to lead the good life?" Keigh asked.

"Will the right, hold to good won, rest in love, and move in art," said Confucius. "These are the ways of leading the good life."

Though Keigh had studied much, he found difficulty in understanding immediately what his grandfather told him, and he repeated slowly, trying to understand each:

"Will the right, hold to good won, rest in love, and move in art."

"Yes, think of these, my son. But now I must get back to my work."

Confucius went on with his work. But not for very long. For in 478 B.C., Confucius died.

When the news became known, his death was mourned all over the Chinese Empire. Even the rulers, who had neglected him during his life, paid homage to his memory.

Many of his pupils and followers mourned his death for three years as if he had been their own father. A number of them even built small shelters near Confucius' grave and remained there all the days of their mourning, studying his teachings.

9. CLOSE TO THE TREE FALLS ITS FRUIT

When Confucius died, Keigh set to work to collect the sayings and lessons he had learned from his grandfather.

Keigh was a poor man, but he gave all his time to the book, which was on THE DOCTRINE OF THE MIDDLE-PATH as taught by Confucius.

To support himself whilst working on the book, Keigh taught pupils who came to him.

"Look, teacher," his pupils would sometimes say to him, "your coat is old and going to pieces, and you have so little to eat!"

"The Master said," Keigh would reply, always calling Confucius 'The Master' and never 'My Grandfather,' "the Master said that a scholar in search of the truth who is ashamed of poor clothes and poor food is not worth talking to."

Sometimes Keigh did not have enough to eat, and then his friends would send him food. Such food as he needed to keep soul and body together he thankfully accepted. But wine and luxuries of dried meat he refused to take. Even the rice and vegetables that he accepted he took only from people whom he respected.

Once a rich man, who heard that Confucius' grandson was in need, sent him food and clothing. Having been told how careful Keigh was in accepting gifts, he sent a servant along with the gifts to give Keigh this message:

"When I borrow from a man, I forget it; when I give a thing, I part with it as freely as if I threw it away."

The servant returned with the gifts saying that Keigh would not accept them.

"Did he give you any reasons?" the rich man asked.

"No," the servant replied.

The rich man then went to Keigh and asked him:

"I have plenty, and you have not. Why will you not accept my gifts?"

"You give away your things as if you were throwing them into a ditch," Keigh replied. "Poor as I am, I cannot think of my body as a ditch. That is why I cannot accept your gifts."

In that way the grandson of Confucius taught the Chinese that they who give charity should have sympathy, and they who take charity should have self-respect.

Keigh went on with his work, happy to see the fame of his grandfather's teachings travelling all over China.

10. MANG-KI-TZE, CALLED MENCIUS

A little over a hundred years after the death of Confucius a child was born in Lu, and he was named Mang.

The many rulers of China were still selfish and unjust as in the days of Confucius, and when Mang grew up, he began to teach against the Princes and Ministers who thought only of their own good and not of the good of the people they were ruling.

Mang gathered about him many pupils and taught them the wisdom of Confucius, which we call *Confucianism*.

His pupils called Mang, Mang-tze, meaning: Mang the Philosopher. We call him *Mencius*.

Mencius went to the ruler of Lu and asked him to rule the land according to the teachings of Confucius. But the Duke of Lu refused to listen to him. So Mencius gathered a number of his followers and started out over the Empire in search of a ruler who would be willing to govern his people as Confucius taught.

Wherever Mencius came he was received with great respect, for his fame as a philosopher was known all over the land.

"What is this Just and Wise rule you are teaching?" the Dukes would ask him.

"What I teach is nothing new. The Master Confucius taught it before me. A just ruler governs his people according to the Five Constant Virtues as taught by the Master."

"And what are the Five Constant Virtues?"

"The Five Constant Virtues are:

BENEVOLENCE—to desire to work for the good of the people;

RIGHTEOUSNESS—not to do unto others what you would not they should do unto you;

PROPRIETY—to always behave with courtesy toward the people you rule;

WISDOM—to let knowledge and understanding be your guides;

SINCERITY—to have sincerity in all you do, for without sincerity, according to the Master, the world cannot exist.

"These are the Five Constant Virtues a ruler ought to follow!"

The Dukes and Princes listened to what Mencius had to say, but none took his advice. And Mencius moved on to other Provinces.

For twenty years he travelled about in that way. And though he failed to find one Prince or Duke who would follow his advice, he succeeded in spreading the teachings of Confucius. And each place he left, he left it with a greater love for the wisdom of the Master.

The growing love and understanding of Confucius amongst the people encouraged Mencius to go on with his work of spreading Confucianism.

Mencius died at the age of eighty-three, nearly 2300 years ago. But his memory is worshipped by millions of people to this day.

The Chinese call Confucius: The First Sage of China. And Mencius is remembered as: The Second Sage of China.

11. THE CRIMINAL OF TEN THOUSAND GENERATIONS

The injustice and selfishness of all the Dukes and Princes and their Ministers all over China became worse and worse as time went on.

Until, about two hundred and fifty years after Confucius died, a new Emperor came to the Throne of China who decided to make a complete change in the government. This Emperor was named Ts'in Shih Hwang-ti. Though he was only a young boy when he came to the throne, he made up his mind to take over the power of the entire country into his own hands.

Of course the Dukes in all the Provinces did not like that. But Ts'in went out north and south and conquered all the people that opposed him. After he had gathered all the power of China into his own hands, he proclaimed himself as The First Emperor.

There had been many, many Emperors in China before him, but Ts'in called himself the First Emperor to show the people that he wished them to forget all the old rulers that had come before him.

It was as if the people had played a game on a blackboard until the slate was all marked up and the players began to cheat badly. Then the boy Emperor Ts'in came along, wiped the board clean, and told the people to begin playing from the beginning and he would watch to see that there was no cheating going on.

When his victories over those who rebelled against him were complete, the Emperor ordered a great celebration to be made in the Palace, and all the Ministers and the Great Men of the land to be invited.

At the celebration the guests, as was the custom, made speeches, praising the Emperor and wishing him a long life.

The Superintendent of Sports arose and said:

"Happy is the Kingdom of China under Your Majesty, Great Emperor Ts'in Shih Hwang-ti! Before you the Empire was broken and weak, but by your strength and wisdom you have united the Empire and made it strong. Before you our Empire was small. Now, through your wisdom, it is so great that wherever the sun and moon shine, there people bow to your authority. This happy Empire that Your Majesty organized will last in happiness for ten thousand generations! From the oldest days there has been no Emperor so great as Your Majesty!"

This speech pleased the Emperor. But then the great scholar Shun-yu Yue arose and said:

"The Superintendent of Sports shows himself a flatterer and therefore he is not a loyal Minister. In order to please Your Majesty, he has slandered the memory of our Great Ancestors, the Emperors of the past."

Everybody around the tables began to murmur about the daring words of the scholar.

One Minister arose and said:

"What you did, Your Majesty, is indeed more than a mere scholar can understand. These scholars do not understand what we are doing today. They only study what people did in the past and long ago. Now that Your Majesty has made our Empire great, these scholars teach amongst the people what is against your wish.

"The best way to keep these scholars from doing Your Majesty any harm is to burn their books and the books written by the scholars of old. And all the scholars who teach them against your will should be put to death."

The young Emperor Ts'in liked the Minister's proposal. He sent out officers all over the land to gather the books of the Great Masters, especially the works of Confucius, his grandson Keigh, and his follower Mencius, and to have them all burned so that the memory of those scholars would be forgotten by the people.

Books in China, in those days, were not written on paper as they are today. They were written on slips of bamboo about one inch wide and two feet long, and the writing was done with a sort of varnish. These slips of bamboo were bound together by punching holes in the corners and fastening them with cords of silk or leather, very much in the same way that we keep loose-leaf books today. Naturally those books were very big and very heavy. A book like the one you are now reading would weigh about one hundred pounds in bamboo slips.

All these heavy books from the Royal Libraries and the private homes began to be gathered not far from the Palace of the Emperor to be burned.

That year, 212 B.C., was a sad year in China. Some of the officers and some of the scholars who loved the Great Works of their Masters, stole copies of the books and walled them into buildings where they could not be found.

But most of the books were burned.

For three whole months the fires blazed not far from the Royal Palace. Day and night the flames were fed with bamboo books, and people from all parts of the country gathered near the great fire, watching the flames throw huge shadows upon the Royal Palace.

After the books were burned, the Emperor ordered that the old scholars who had memorized the books and were teaching them should be put to death. About five hundred scholars were killed, and hundreds of others were either driven out of the country, or put to work on the Great Wall of China that was then being built.

Several years later, when Emperor Ts'in died, the people took out the books that had been hidden in the walls and made a great holiday to celebrate the memory of Confucius and his followers, and the books that had been saved.

The name of Confucius, which Emperor Ts'in wanted the people to forget, had become dearer than ever to them. And the memory of Ts'in was hated.

Emperor Ts'in, after whose name we call his land China (Ts'in-a), wanted to be remembered by his people as the best Emperor in ten thousand generations. But instead the people of China remember him as:

The Criminal of Ten Thousand Generations.

Part Two: TAOISM

THE RELIGION FEW CAN UNDERSTAND

Lao-tze wrote:

> "To those who are good to
> me I am good; and to those
> who are not good to me I am
> good. And thus all get to be
> good."

FOUNDED: 6th Century B.C.

FOUNDER: Lao-tze (The Old Philosopher). Consider-
able confusion exists about the founder of Taoism;
and some even question whether he ever existed. According to one legend his real name was Li Erh, and
he was presumably born in 604 B.C., and presumably
died in 524 B.C.

PLACE: China

SACRED BOOK: *Tao-Teh-King* (The Book of Reason
and Virtue), is the shortest of all the Sacred Books in
the world. It is presumably written by Lao-tze late in
life; and though it contains only about 5,000 words,
it is so obscure that it is the subject of many and long
volumes.

NUMBER OF ADHERENTS: 50,000,000; but this figure
is at best very general, since a Taoist may also be a
Buddhist or a Confucian.

DISTRIBUTION: China, Korea, and Manchuria

TAOISTS IN THE UNITED STATES: 10,000 to 15,000

SECTS: Since Taoism is a mystical religion, its interpr
tations are many and its sects are many.

TAOISM:

The Religion Few Can Understand

1. THE MEETING OF THE TWO PHILOSOPHERS

At the time the fame of Confucius began spreading over China, early in his career as a teacher, there was another philosopher whose name was upon the lips of many admirers.

Confucius had heard of this philosopher, called Lao-tze, who lived in the city of Lo-yang, and worked there as Keeper of the Archives in the Imperial Library. The teachings of Lao-tze seemed very strange to Confucius, and later when he was invited to the Imperial Library to study the manuscripts of ancient Chinese Music, Confucius sent word to Lao-tze that he wished to meet him.

After the messenger left, Confucius seated himself on a mat, and began to read a manuscript written on bamboo slips. As he sat there studying, he heard someone coming into the room. He looked up and saw a bald-headed, long-bearded old man coming towards him. Confucius immediately rose to show due respect to his elder.

"What are you reading, Sir?" the old man asked.

"The Book of the Changes," Confucius replied, realizing that the very old man before him was none other than Lao-tze himself. Then he added: "The sages of old studied this book I am told."

"For what purpose do you read it?" asked Lao-tze.

"The Book of the Changes teaches about humanity and justice."

"Humanity and justice!" Lao-tze exclaimed impatiently, and began to pace the room. "Does the pigeon bathe itself all day to make itself white? It does not. It is naturally white. And so with people. If they are good and just at heart you do not need to teach them justice."

This began a long discussion between the two philosophers, Lao-tze doing most of the talking. From time to time he asked Confucius questions to which Confucius replied very politely.

"Why do you study so much about things that were

done in the olden days? Of what interest and benefit is that to you?" Lao-tze asked.

"I believe," Confucius replied to the old man, "that people are born good, and that learning and knowledge will keep them good. But before we can have new knowledge, we must first know the old. That is why I think the wisdom of our forefathers should be studied carefully."

This reply angered Lao-tze.

"The men of whom you speak, Sir, together with their bones have mouldered in the grave. Let go of your proud airs, and your big plans to teach the world justice. All this is of no use to you. That is what I have to tell you, and that is all!"

Then he turned and left the room.

Later, when Confucius returned to his followers, they all asked eagerly about his meeting with Lao-tze and what he thought of him. Confucius thought for a while, then said:

"I know how the birds fly, how fish swim, and how animals run. And the runner may be snared, the swimmer may be hooked, and the flyer may be shot with an arrow. But there is the dragon. I cannot tell how it mounts on the wind through the clouds and rises to heaven. Today I have seen Lao-tze, and I can only compare him to the dragon."

The followers of Confucius understood from his reply that their Master had been greatly impressed by Lao-tze whom he did not understand any more than how the dragon goes to heaven.

Who, then, was this greatly respected, angry old man, Lao-tze? What did he teach, and what do we know about him?

2. WHAT WE KNOW ABOUT LAO-TZE

In the village of Keuh-Jin, in the parish of Le, in the District of Tsow, there lived a poor man named Li. Li was a very poor man, but he was married. And in the Third Year of the Twenty-First Sovereign of the Dynasty of Chow, which was really about 2530 years ago, Li's wife gave birth to a boy whom they named Li-Peh-Yang.

We know little about Li-Peh-Yang's young days. But we do know that at an early age he became Keeper of the Royal Archives in the city called Lo-yang. And

Keeper of the Royal Archives in Lo-yang he remained for many years.

His work in the Imperial Library gave Li-Peh-Yang an opportunity to study a great deal. When he later began to express his opinions on philosophy and religion, he gained the respect and admiration of many who named him Lao-tze, meaning: The Old Philosopher.

But fame did not change Lao-tze's life. Keeper of the Royal Archives he was, and Keeper of the Royal Archives he remained. In the Imperial Library he might have stayed to the end of his long life, had not the rulers of his Province become worse from day to day.

When the rulers became so selfish and dishonorable that the Old Philosopher felt it was an insult to live under their rule, he decided to leave the place where he had lived almost all his life. He was ninety years old then. But he made up his mind to leave the Royal Library, leave Lo-yang, and leave the Province he had lived in and that was his home.

And he left.

When he got as far as the border of the Province, the Guardian of the Border recognized the Old Philosopher and he would not let him pass.

"Why will you not let me pass?" Lao-tze asked.

"Master, you are a great philosopher," the Guardian of the Border replied. "Your fame is known everywhere. And yet you have never written down your teachings. If you should leave us now we would not have even a record of your teachings."

"If I write down my teachings will you let me pass?" Lao-tze asked.

"Yes, Master!"

Lao-tze sat down right there and then and wrote down the most important parts of his teachings. He wrote a little book of about twenty-five pages, which he named:

TAO-TEH-KING, which might be translated to mean: THE BOOK OF REASON AND VIRTUE.

This little book he gave to the Guardian of the Border, and he was then permitted to leave the Province.

Lao-tze left, and was never heard of again.

This is all we know of the Old Philosopher.

About Confucius we know so many things. We know where he lived, and how he lived, and what he did all his life, and how he did it. We even know what food he liked;

how he received guests; and even how he slept. But of Lao-tze we know almost nothing.

When we place side by side what we know of Confucius and what we know of Lao-tze, they might be compared to two statues in an old museum:

One statue, that of Confucius, stands right in the sunlight where we can see it very clearly. But the second, that of Lao-tze, is like a statue that stands in a far, dark corner where it looks more like a shadow than anything real.

The only proof that we have that the shadowy Lao-tze was real is the little book which he wrote at the age of ninety, just before he disappeared.

Many books ten times, a hundred times as large as the *Tao-Teh-King* were written in China, and elsewhere, that have long been forgotten.

Why then is this little book by Lao-tze remembered? What does this Old Philosopher teach that his small book should have survived these many hundreds of years?

3. THE TAO-TEH-KING

The *Tao-Teh-King* is a little book, but it is packed full of thoughts. Some of these thoughts are easy to understand. Some of them are hard to understand. And some of them are impossible to understand.

To begin with, Lao-tze teaches that *Tao* is the Great Beginning of all things in the world, and that people who want to lead the good life must follow *Tao*.

But what this *Tao* is we are never clearly told. The word 'Tao' gives all the translators a great deal of trouble. Some say it means The Way.

Others say it means, The Path.

Some say it means, Reason.

Some say it means, The Word.

And some say it means, God.

Lao-tze tells us himself that we can never learn anything about this *Tao,* if we do not already know all about it.

"They who know do not tell, and they who tell do not know," he wrote in his little book.

If we don't know what *Tao* is, we can never learn anything about it from those who do know. And yet it is this *Tao,* about which we can never learn anything, unless we know it already, that is the most important thing in life.

Confucius, too, did not claim to know anything about God in Heaven. But he taught that people should try to be good, and God would take care of Himself.

Lao-tze taught just the very opposite. He taught that the first duty of people who want to lead the good life was to believe in *Tao* (the Way or God), and the world will take care of itself.

Confucius taught that people are born good; Lao-tze also taught that people are born good. But Confucius said that people can be kept good through being properly educated. Whereas Lao-tze believed that it was not necessary for people to learn anything.

"They who know *Tao* are not very learned," he wrote. "The very learned do not know *Tao.*"

Which might mean that good people ought to be ignorant. This, of course, could not be exactly what the Old Philosopher meant. But just what he really meant by such sayings is hard to tell, and no one really knows.

But besides these sayings that are not very clear, his little book also has some very clear and very good ideas. One of these is against war:

"The great object of the Good Man is to keep peace. He takes no pleasure in winning battles, and in killing his fellow men."

Not only is Lao-tze against killing people in war, he is even against killing criminals as a punishment for their crimes. By killing criminals, he said, people are not made any better and crime is not done away with. The only way to make people good, he wrote, is by treating them with kindness at all times.

"*To those who are good to me I am good,*" he wrote in his little book. "*And to those who are not good to me I am also good. And thus all get to be good. To those who are sincere with me I am sincere; and to those who are not sincere with me I am sincere. And thus all come to be sincere.*"

And later he wrote:

"*A truly good man loves all men and hates none.*"

These passages, which are easy to understand, are not many in his book. Most of the *Tao-Teh-King* is not very clear.

And so, when we place, side by side, the teachings of Confucius and the teachings of Lao-tze, we can again compare them to two statues in an old museum:

The teachings of Confucius are in the light and we can understand them very easily. He teaches:

That people ought not to worry about God in Heaven and about Life after Death;

That people are born good, and they ought to remain good as long as they live;

That the way to remain good, the way to lead the good life, should be through: Knowledge; Ancestor-Worship; Loyalty of children to their parents; Loyalty of citizens to their rulers; and, above all things, Justice.

These teachings of Confucius are all very easy to understand.

But the teachings of the Old Philosopher are hidden in shadows. We rarely know exactly what he means and what he wishes us to understand by what he says.

Yet this little book became the foundation of a religion.

This religion is called TAOISM, which means, the Religion of the Way, or the Religion of God.

And the Sacred Scriptures of Taoism is the *Tao-Teh-King*.

4. THE IDOLS OF TAOISM

Supposing people were to find a book and open it and read:

"Repay injury with kindness; repay evil with good. Abracadabra, his puff but a piff. *If people are hard to govern it is because they are too wise.* Fisk, lobster short and long."

And supposing the book were just full of such writing. One would think that people, finding such a book, would read those parts that had meaning, and, if the parts were really good, they would remember them. And they would forget all the rest that had no meaning at all.

Just so, one would think the followers of Lao-tze would have taken out the beautiful and good parts of the *Tao-Teh-King* and would have forgotten all the rest.

That is *not* what they did.

They did the *very opposite.*

That which is good and beautiful in the *Tao-Teh-King*

they forgot, and those parts that made almost no meaning, the abracadabra parts, they remembered.

But since no one could understand them, they set to work and wrote long books explaining the meaning of those parts that made no meaning.

Then came others after them who wrote books explaining the explanation.

And their followers wrote explanations, explaining the explanations of the explanations of the *Tao-Teh-King*.

Until, after two or three hundred years, the followers of Taoism did not study the work of Lao-tze, but spent much time and energy studying the explanations that explained the explanations of the explainers who explained the first explanations of the *Tao-Teh-King*.

And most of these dizzy explanations explained something that the Old Philosopher, Lao-tze, never thought of, never dreamt of, and never wrote about in his book.

For instance, some explained that somewhere far away there was an island in the sea so wonderful that anyone setting foot on it would live forever and ever. And on that wonderful island there was a river, and anyone who bathed in that river would remain young forever and ever.

Since these Taoists could not find that wonderful island and that wonderful river, they hoped to be able to invent a pill or a medicine that would make people live forever and remain always young.

They also explained that anyone who can understand the *Tao-Teh-King* should have no difficulty in turning pig-iron into gold and silver.

We have seen before how the teachings of great men are often misunderstood and explained in the wrong way by their followers. We have seen how Prince Gautama the Buddha taught his followers not to believe in idols, and later they made an idol of the Buddha himself. We saw how Prince Mahavira taught his followers that there was no god whom people ought to worship, and later his followers made a sort of god of Mahavira along with twenty-three other Jinas.

But no great teacher of the past was so misunderstood and so wrongly explained as the Old Philosopher, Lao-tze.

Lao-tze, in that part of his little book that we can understand, taught people to live simply, to do away with war, and to follow the Godly Way. But his followers ex-

plained his ideas to mean that they ought to find some
hidden secret as to how people could become young and
live forever.

About five hundred years after the *Tao-Teh-King* was
written one Taoist, named Chang-Tao-ling, was said to
have discovered a drink that would make people live
forever.

Immediately the Taoists began to worship him. And
to this day his great-great-grandchildren are worshipped.
Their leader, the descendant of Chang-Tao-ling, is called
the Pearly Emperor, and he lives in the Dragon-Tiger
Mountains near Kiang-si, and rules his followers with the
power of a king.

Besides the Pearly Emperor, the Taoists worship many
idols. They worship Dragons of every kind. And they
worship Rats, Weasels, and Snakes.

They believe that if they carry certain ashes, or certain
stones, or certain writings on them, then bullets cannot
kill them, water cannot drown them, and fire cannot burn
them.

As time went on their belief in devils, demons, nixies,
pixies, vampires, gnomes, goblins, and every other variety
of evil spirit became very common.

Millions of Taoists in China still believe in them. When
they eat and when they drink, when they walk and when
they rest, and in whatever they do, they think about these
evil-spirits who, they believe, are about everywhere to
do them harm.

5. THE MAN WHO KILLED A DEVIL

There are many ways in which to keep the evil-spirits
away, and to protect oneself from them, the Taoists
believe.

When a Taoist walks through the forest, he either sings
or he whistles because he believes that his music keeps
the wood-devils from coming near him. The wood-devils
dislike music just as mosquitoes dislike smoke.

In some Chinese houses, even after one enters, one has
to turn around in a sort of crooked foyer before entering
the first room. This arrangement is made especially for
the evil-spirits, so that if an evil-spirit should rush into
the house, he would dash against the wall and be killed.

Some Chinese houses have paintings of forests and

jungles where our entrance-door would be. That makes the fronts of their houses very beautiful. But that is not why those paintings are there. Those paintings are there for the evil-spirits, who might try to get into the house. But as they come rushing up and try to get into what they think is the entrance, they dash into the painted woods and jungles and are never heard of again.

The worst evil-spirits, they believe, are to be found in the mountains. All the mountains have their evil-spirits. The bigger the mountains, of course, the stronger their spirits.

Thousands of stories about these mountain-devils are told in China. Sometimes people get the better of these evil-spirits of the mountains. And here is a story to prove it:

Beneath the mountain Li-lu there was once an inn. Travellers passing by there would stop to rest. But if any traveller stayed there overnight, the evil-spirit of Li-lu would come down with fifty devils dressed up as men and women, and would kill him.

One day Pih-He the Magician came to that Inn and decided to stay there overnight. He knew about the place, but Pih-He was a great magician and was not afraid.

Pih-He arrived early in the afternoon and made himself comfortable. And when it became dark, he lit a candle and began to read such writings as were good for keeping evil-spirits away.

There sat Pih-He by the candle light, all alone.

One hour passed.

Another hour passed.

The tallow of the candle began to drip, and the candle began to grow shorter and shorter.

Exactly at midnight the door opened and ten tall men dressed in black came in and sat down near Pih-He. And without saying a word they began to gamble. The magician pretended he did not see them.

But as he sat there reading he took out a little magic mirror and looked into it.

What he saw in the mirror made his teeth chatter. For in the little magic mirror he saw ten dogs sitting close together and gambling. Pih-He looked quickly, and there were the ten men gambling. He looked into the mirror again, and there he saw the dogs again.

Pih-He now knew who those gamblers were, but he wanted to make certain. So he picked up his candle and began to walk up and down the room still pretending to read.

But as he walked up and down he came nearer and nearer the gamblers.

When he came very close to them he suddenly pushed the candle right against one of them. Immediately Pih-He smelled the burning of hair.

The Magician quickly drew out a knife and threw it at the gambler. The other gamblers jumped up and ran away, but the gambler Pih-He had singed with the candle fell to the ground.

When Pih-He bent over to see whether he had killed him, he saw a dead dog lying on the ground.

6. WHY TAOISM FOUND MANY FOLLOWERS

About a hundred years after the *Tao-Teh-King* was written, one Taoist leader wrote a book in which he said:

"Passing through solid metal or stone, walking in the midst of fire or on the surface of water—all these things are possible to him who is in harmony with *Tao.*"

Such teachings of magic became worse and worse as time went on. Millions of ignorant Chinese began to believe in these things and feared the magicians and the priests who claimed that they had power over the evil-spirits. Yet the number of followers of Taoism grew rapidly.

The reason so many Chinese became Taoists and believed in its teachings is not very hard to understand:

Long, long ago the Chinese were Nature-Worshippers. In those far-off days they believed that all things in nature had spirits.

Later they divided the spirits of nature into two groups: the good-spirits who did good things for people, they called *Shen;* and the evil-spirits they called *Kwei.*

The Chinese had not forgotten their old religion, and parts of it are still to be found amongst them to this day. To this day they believe in the good work of the *Shen*, the good-spirits, and the evil work of *Kwei*, the bad-spirits.

But even the *Shen*, the good-spirits, sometimes stop being good. The good-spirit of rain, for instance, sometimes does not give rain when they need it. That, the Chinese believe, is because the good-spirit of rain has fallen asleep. In order to wake him up they make a huge dragon out of paper and wood, painted in many bright colors. This dragon represents the good-spirit of rain. They carry the dragon through the streets and sing aloud to wake him up.

But if he does not wake up, they threaten to beat him.

Sometimes, if it does not rain, they actually beat and tear up this dragon. Sometimes they try to bribe the dragon by promising to give him a great title. And if it rains within a given time, they keep their promise.

When Taoism began to teach about so many evil-spirits and about magic, the people, who still remembered their old beliefs in many spirits, were ready to listen to the Magicians and the stories of wonder told about the Pearly Emperor.

7.   BUDDHISM IN CHINA

For about five hundred years after the death of Confucius, Taoism and Confucianism were the two religions of China.

When Emperor Ts'in ordered the books of Confucius and his followers to be burned, he allowed the Taoists' writings to be saved. Emperor Ts'in himself hoped to find the magic pill that would make him live forever and rule China forever. That was one of the reasons he encouraged the Taoist teachings in his day. But after his death the followers of Confucius became the strongest power in China.

Meanwhile Chinese merchants travelling to Nepal and India, came back with marvelous stories of a Prince named Gautama.

As the years passed the more marvelous became the tales these Chinese merchants told of Prince Gautama and his teachings. The stories they told travelled all over China. And the people repeated them to each other in great admiration of the far-away Prince.

The Chinese, as we have seen, are, and always have been, *Ancestor-Worshippers*. To them the dead are almost as real as the living. Naturally they wanted to know what happened to their forefathers after their death.

Neither Taoism nor Confucianism answered those questions about life after death for them. When the Chinese heard of a religion that explained about life after death, and about Nirvana, they wanted to know all about it.

And so the teachings of the Buddha, very much changed by his followers, slowly became known all over China.

About five hundred years after the death of Confucius, Emperor Ming Ti became a Buddhist and he ordered the *Tripitaki,* the Sacred Scriptures of Buddhism, to be translated into Chinese and taught to the people.

The followers of Confucius, who were many in the land, fought the Hindu religion very bitterly. But after years of fighting, Buddhism won. It spread all over the country and became rooted there like an oak tree. The Chinese people wanted a religion that would explain to them things neither Taoism nor Confucianism explained. And Buddhism was just such a religion.

By accepting Buddhism the people of China did not give up the other two religions. They only added another. The Buddha (whom the Chinese call Omito Fo) was added to the company of their beloved Confucius and Lao-tze.

The Chinese today are talked of as a people who follow "The Three Teachings." These are the teachings of Confucius, Lao-tze, and the Buddha.

And sometimes one Chinese follows all three of them.

Buddhism has the greatest number of followers. But the Buddhist influence upon the people of China is not as great as the influence of Confucianism.

8. CONFUCIANISM TODAY

The chief reason why the Chinese people accepted Buddhism was because it explained to them things they wanted to know about death and about heaven.

But people do not spend all their time thinking of what happens to their souls after death. People also eat, drink, and sleep. They spend their time making shoes, hats, and clothes to wear. They build houses to live in, because they cannot live like monkeys in the trees. They prepare food to eat. They sing songs and play lutes when happy. They write books and paint pictures. They tell stories. They travel. They buy and sell. They bathe. They swim. They play games. They eat sweets which they like very much. And they do many, many other things that have nothing to do with thinking of death or what happens after death.

If we could put side by side the time the Chinese spend in thinking of God and worrying about what becomes of their souls after death, and the time they spend in doing all the other things, it would look very much like a small red cherry placed near a big, big pumpkin.

And if Confucius did not tell his people anything about the cherry, he did tell them much about the pumpkin. Though he told them nothing about God and Heaven, he did tell them what to do in order to make out of the pumpkin very delicious pumpkin-pie. Confucius told his people how to live and how to do things that would make them happy and good.

But in teaching the people how to be happy and good, Confucius did not destroy their old beliefs in the things the Chinese had loved for centuries.

Most important of all he encouraged their belief in *Ancestor-Worship*.

By encouraging Ancestor-Worship Confucius won the hearts of his people.

Confucius travelled a great deal during his lifetime. He met all kinds of people. He met wise men. He met scholars. He met Dukes and Princes. As Minister of Crime he worked with lawyers, judges, and criminals. And during his long life he learned what his people wanted most, what was good for them, and what would make them happy.

He did not worry, as the Taoists did, about turning iron into gold. Because that, he knew, would not make the people any happier. If all the iron in the world were turned into gold, gold would be cheap and iron would be dear. And the people would not be any happier than they are now.

Besides, turning iron into gold was impossible, and what was impossible did not interest Confucius. What he wanted was to make people happy in ways that *were* possible.

So he started out by saying that the first thing people must learn is that no man can live all by himself and be happy.

"From the Emperor downwards, all must have friends," he said.

We must have food to eat, clothing to wear, and houses to live in. No one man can make all these things for himself and live by himself and be happy. But when people live together, one man makes shoes, another bakes bread, another prepares food, another builds houses, and then they share what they have. The baker bakes bread and gives it to all the people, and they give him in exchange shoes, clothing, and a house. Or they give him money with which to buy the things he needs, which is really about the same thing.

When people live together in that way, they must also have a government to see that each man does something useful for what he receives, and that no man is permitted to take away anything which he does not earn.

Each family, Confucius taught, ought to be like a little government. The parents take care of their children and give them a good education. And the children respect and obey their parents and do all they can to make them happy.

The duty of children to their parents is one of Confucius' most important teachings, and it is known as HSIAO, which really means:

Honor your father and your mother, do everything you can to make them happy, and worship their memory.

All his teachings Confucius taught in words so simple that everybody could understand them. His own writings and the books he gathered, which are called *The Classics,* became the Holy Scriptures of his followers. But unlike the Holy Scriptures of other religions, *The Classics* became also the books of general education for the people.

In China, if a man wants to become a government official he has to pass an examination on *The Classics.* And in all the schools of China the sayings of Confucius are printed on tablets along the walls, and children learn them as soon as they can read.

The people of China love the memory of Confucius to this day. He is not worshipped as a God, as they worship the Buddha. But he is loved and remembered as the Greatest Chinese Patriot and Sage that ever lived on their soil.

At the age of thirty-four Confucius had over 3000 admirers and followers. Now, after 2400 years, there are over 250,000,000 people in China alone who admire him.

The wise men of the land sing and praise him:

"Great art thou, O Perfect Sage!

Thy virtue is full, thy teaching complete!

Amongst mortal men thère has not yet been thine equal!"

The common people who cannot find great enough words with which to praise him, exclaim:

"Confucius, Confucius! How great art thou, Confucius!"

Part Three: SHINTO

THE WAY OF THE GODS

> "The ways of shining Heaven
> are far:
> Turn thee! Ah! turn to things
> yet near;
> Turn to thy earthly home,
> O friend!
> And try to do thy duty here."
>
> Omi Okura

FOUNDED: Prehistoric

FOUNDER: Unknown

PLACE: Japan

SACRED BOOKS: *Kojiki* (Records of the Ancients), *Nihongi* (Chronicles of Japan), and a later work *Yengishiki* (Hymns and Prayers), are the works used by the followers of Shinto, but they are not regarded as Sacred Books in the same way as we regard our Bible.

NUMBER OF ADHERENTS: About 30,000,000. But followers of Shinto may be at the same time adherents of Buddhism, or Christianity, or Taoism.

DISTRIBUTION: Asia, most in Japan

SHINTO:

The Way of the Gods

1. WHEN JAPAN WAS VERY YOUNG

If you look at a map of Asia you will see a strange looking swan swimming towards a school of minnows with some larger fish amongst them.

The body of the swan is, mostly, China.

Its big red bill is Korea.

And the many small and big fish are the Islands of Japan, known as the Land of the Rising Sun.

There are over four thousand islands in the Japanese Kingdom, and about five hundred of these are inhabited by people. There are no great rivers nor vast plains on these islands, but they have many high mountains and many deep valleys.

And there amongst the mountains and the valleys of Japan, always in fear of the frequent earthquakes, lives a race of people who look very much like the Chinese, paint pictures and play musical instruments like those of the Chinese, make statues and lacquered ornaments like those of their nearest neighbors, and believe in religions very much like those believed in in China.

The reason the Japanese writing, music, and religions are so much like those of China is very easy to explain:

That is where almost all these things came from in the first place.

Japan borrowed her writing, her arts, and her religions from China. Or rather, China sent them across, through Korea, as her gifts to young Japan. For Japan, as compared with India and China, is a very young country.

When India had already such great men at Prince Mahavira, the Jaina, and Prince Gautama, the Buddha, making changes in their old religion, Japan was still a group of wild islands inhabited by several clans of savage people fighting with each other in the most uncivilized way. And when China was already so old as to have books of Philosophy and books of Ceremony, telling people just exactly how to receive guests and how to dress

when going to Temple, the Japanese were still a simple
and primitive people who lived by catching fish and hunting wild game for food.

The Chinese, then, called the Japanese 'Dwarfs,' and
described them as people who tattooed their faces, and
who fought with spears and bows and arrows.

When the Chinese began to send across their art of
writing and their art of making musical instruments, their
ideas of how to grow rice and how to make silk from the
spinnings of the silkworm, the Japanese were very glad
to receive all these wonderful gifts, and were very eager
to learn.

From the beginning of their history, up to the present
day, the Japanese have always been good pupils, and
learned very quickly anything that was of interest to
them. When the Japanese received their knowledge of
writing, of agriculture, of the arts, and of religions from
China, they changed all of these very much to fit their
climate and their lives which were quite different from
the Chinese.

But even before the cultured Chinese brought their
gifts to Japan, even before the Japanese learned to write,
or to play musical instruments, they already had a religion.

In so far as we know there are no people, no matter
how savage and uncivilized, who had or have no religion
whatsoever.

So, too, the Japanese of over 2000 years ago had a
religion.

The religion was later, much later, named *Kamino-
Michi*.

But it is better known by its Chinese name:

SHINTO.

We have seen that the early Chinese believed in good
spirits and evil spirits, and the good spirits were called
SHEN. And the teachings of the Old Philosopher Lao-tze
were called TAO, meaning The Way.

So SHINTO (Shen-Tao) must mean in Chinese, and
does mean: *The Way of the Good Spirits*.

2. THE WAY OF THE GOOD SPIRITS

To the Japanese of over 2000 years ago the world was a
very small place. They believed that they were the only

people on earth, and their kingdom, which they called The Great-Eight-Island-Land, was the entire earth, surrounded by water and small islands. Even the sky, they believed, was very near to them.

So near was the sky to Japan, they believed, that long, long ago an arrow that was sent up from the earth pierced through the sky and made a hole in it. Through that hole in the sky came falling down to earth the trees, bushes, herbs, and all the living creatures. All things on earth came, in that way, from the sky called Heaven.

Since all these things on earth came from Heaven, one would conclude that Heaven was filled with just the same things that one sees on earth.

That was exactly what the Japanese of long ago believed.

They believed that life in Heaven was very much the same as in Japan, only much nicer.

They also believed that there was a world right under the earth where there was also life and people as on the earth, only it was not as nice.

The entrance to the Underworld was open once upon a time so that people on earth could go down there for a visit. But one day an earthquake closed the entrance to the Underworld with a big stone.

Long ago there was also a bridge to Heaven and people could go up there, too, for a visit. But that bridge broke down and was never, never mended again.

In those days the religion of the Japanese was very simple. They had no images, they had no sacred books, they had no commandments, and they had no priests. Like the early Chinese, they believed that the stars, the moon, the sun, the mountains, the rivers, the thunder and the rain all had spirits that could do good or evil if they wanted to, and to make them do good they had to be worshipped. Therefore the Japanese worshipped all these things.

If they wanted rain, they went out to the river and prayed to the river to give them rain. If they wanted the rain to stop and the sun to shine, they would go out and pray to the sun.

Of all the early religions in the world we know of, there is none quite so simple as Shintoism was in those days in Japan.

Besides worshipping nature, the Japanese also worshipped their *Mikado*. To the Japanese their Mikado is not a human being like themselves, but he is more like the Sun, the Moon, or Mount Fuji. He is a being that, like the gods, must be worshipped.

Why the Japanese worshipped, and still worship, their Mikado, is explained in the *Kojiki* and the *Nihongi* (The Records of the Ancient Masters, and The Record of Japan), that were written about 1300 years ago.

After the world was formed, so the story in these Sacred Books tells, there were many gods and spirits. And in the Seventh Generation of the Gods lived Izanagi and Izanami, who were also gods.

One day Izanagi and Izanami stood upon the Floating Bridge of Heaven talking to each other.

"I wonder what is down below us," said Izanagi.

"I wonder," said Izanami.

So Izanagi took the Jewel-Spear of Heaven, lowered it into the air and swung it around as a blind man might swing his cane in a strange place. Suddenly the spear splashed into a mighty ocean.

When Izanagi raised the Jewel-Spear of Heaven the salty water dripped from it and, dried by the wind, became hard and formed an island in the middle of the sea.

"Let us go down and live on that island," said Izanagi.

"Let us go down," said Izanami.

And so they went down from the Floating Bridge of Heaven to live on that island. There they created the Great-Eight-Island-Land, and there they gave birth to The Three Noble Children: The Sun-Goddess, and her brothers, the Moon-God and the Storm-God.

The Sun-Goddess, called *Amaterasu-Omi-Kami*, also had a family. And her grandson, Jimmu Tenno, became the First Emperor of Japan.

That is why the Japanese worship their Mikado. To this day they believe that their Mikado is a great-great-great-grandson, the one hundred and twenty-fourth grandson, of the Sun-Goddess *Amaterasu-Omi-Kami*.

By teaching that the Mikado was the grandson of the Sun-Goddess, the old religion of Japan, Shintoism, made its followers believe that it was their religious duty to be loyal to their ruler. And by teaching them to worship the mountains and the valley of Japan, Shintoism made its followers great lovers of their country.

In this manner, the old religion of Japan joined Patriotism and Religion into one. And even today the National Flag of Japan has upon it a red sun to show that theirs is the Land of the Rising Sun where once lived the Sun-Goddess *Amaterasu*.

3.   PRINCE GAUTAMA ARRIVES IN JAPAN

Early in their history the Japanese learned from the Chinese how to cultivate the land and grow rice, how to take care of the silk-worm and make silk, how to write, how to paint, and how to do many other things.

And whilst the Japanese learned from China how to *do things,* they also learned from them how *to think* and what *to believe*.

The teachings of Confucius, the Great Sage of China, came to them and taught them Ancestor-Worship.

Not only did China send across to Japan the teachings of their own Confucius, but when Buddhism, the Religion that came to them from India, became very strongly rooted in China, they sent out missionaries farther East, through Korea and Japan.

The King of Korea, about 1300 years ago, was a Buddhist. And he sent to the Mikado of Japan an image of the Buddha made of pure gold. Some of the Buddhist Sacred Books came with it.

The Mikado, to show his reverence for these gifts, had a temple built especially for the Golden Buddha and the Sacred Books.

When the temple was built, the Korean King sent Buddhist priests to Japan to explain their religion.

And so the Buddha arrived in Japan as a gift from one King to another.

But it was not the Buddhism that had left India about a thousand years before. When the teachings of the Buddha left home they taught people to live simply, to follow the Eight-fold Path, to do away with Idol-worship.

As Buddhism travelled over the Himalaya Mountains, over Tibet, through China, through Korea, and into Japan, it was slowly changed by its followers. The Buddha himself became an idol to be worshipped. And many idols were added to surround him.

The Buddha left home as a beggar, and arrived in Japan as a Prince. And an army of shining idols came before him, and an army of glittering idols followed behind.

When the simple Japanese saw the colorful and rich parade of idols, and heard the wonderful stories of the Buddha's life, they admired it all, and many became Buddhists.

Before very long Buddhism had temples in every town in Japan and became the greatest religion there. It even threatened to drive Shintoism out of the land of its birth.

But Shintoism taught the worship of the Emperor, and so the Emperor helped to keep it alive amongst the people.

Yet more important in saving Shintoism in Japan was the fact that the old religion made friends with Confucianism, and together they worked out rules of how the nobles ought to live. That is known in Japan as BUSHIDO, which means: The Ways of the Knights.

4. THE WAYS OF THE KNIGHTS

Just as China was almost always a peace-loving country, Japan, in the early days of its history, was always at war. They fought with the Koreans, they fought amongst themselves, and they fought their neighbors and enemies farther north.

In a country where there is much war, the soldiers are greatly admired. So in Japan the soldiers, or the Warriors as they called them, became the heroes of the country. And it was an honor to belong to the class of Warriors. The leaders of these Warriors became the Nobles of Japan, called the Knights.

The Knights of Japan were not only patriots and warriors, they were also scholars and gentlemen. These gathered and worked out a sort of manual as to how a man of their class, a Knight, ought to live and how he ought to behave. Confucius, they said, was an Ideal Gentleman. They took his teachings and, with them as their guide, worked out the Rules of Conduct for the Knights. These were called BUSHIDO.

The rules of Bushido are many, but the most important are the *Ten Ways of a Gentleman:*

A Gentleman should love JUSTICE;
A Gentleman should have COURAGE;
A Gentleman should be BENEVOLENT;
A Gentleman is always POLITE;
A Gentleman is HONORABLE;

A Gentleman is LOYAL;
A Gentleman has SELF-CONTROL;
A Gentleman searches for WISDOM;
A Gentleman has LOVE OF LEARNING.

After some time the Rules of Bushido began to be explained in a way they were not meant to be explained. Bushido taught that a Knight ought to be honorable, but the later Knights explained it to mean that a Knight ought to kill himself when his superior officer died. In order to defend his honor each Knight carried a sword whenever he went out of his house. By and by, a Knight did not leave his home without at least two swords dangling at his sides. They began to look upon the sword as sacred and worshipped it.

In 1868, for many political reasons, the entire class of the followers of *Bushido* were done away with by the government of Japan. And five years later they were prohibited from carrying the swords that distinguished them and that were their special mark of honor.

But the influence of the Ten Ways of a Gentleman, as taught by *Bushido,* is still felt in the life of Japan today.

5. IN JAPAN TODAY

When the first golden image of Buddha arrived in Japan there were few people in that land. On all the 4200 islands there were fewer people than in New York City at present. But their numbers grew and grew, and today there are nearly 80,000,000 people under the flag of the Rising Sun.

When the Japanese became a great and powerful nation in the East, people in the West wanted to know all about them. What do these Japanese look like? How do they dress? What are their manners? What do they think?

But few people of the West knew anything about the Japanese. And many went to the islands of Japan to find all these things out for themselves. Some of these travellers in Japan wrote books of what they saw and heard in the Land of the Rising Sun.

In most of the books the travellers tell that the first three things about the Japanese they noticed were:

The Japanese love of nature;
The Japanese love of art;
The Japanese love of learning.

No people in the world, they recorded, are such lovers of nature as the Japanese. They love the mountains, they love the rivers, they love the forests, and, most of all, they love flowers. Children in Japan, when quite young, are taught how to arrange flowers in vases. There are holidays and festivals in their land to celebrate the blooming of some of their trees. And they grow many cherry, plum, and peach trees not so much for their fruit as for their blossoms.

The Japanese love of flowers is equalled by their love of poetry and painting. Not until one has seen the inside of a Japanese home, we are told, can one realize how important art is to them. Their simple homes are arranged beautifully. All those who can afford it, try to own prints of famous paintings. Children are taught to understand what makes a beautiful thing beautiful, and to love it.

But far greater than their love of nature and art is the Japanese love of learning. They have borrowed their knowledge from other nations, but whatever they learn, they change to suit their own particular needs. And the Japanese are always eager to learn new things.

Why the Japanese are so fond of nature, of art, and of learning, few books explain. But the explanation lies in their religions.

The Japanese, like the Chinese, might be said to be followers of "Three Teachings": *Shintoism, Buddhism,* and *Confucianism.*

Through Shintoism the Japanese learned to love nature.
They built their temples to the nature gods high up on the mountain sides, and came there to celebrate various festivals. Dressed in their most beautiful clothes they streamed in gay crowds to these temples in Spring and Autumn. They saw the trees when the first buds of spring began to swell; and they saw them when the autumn painted the leaves with burnt copper and interlined them with dull gold. They saw the rivers overflowing in the spring; and they saw them in the summer when the face of the water was as smooth as the worshipped mirror of *Amatesaru-Omi-Kami,* the Sun Goddess. All these things

in nature they saw from childhood and came to love dearly.

Through Buddhism they learned to love the beautiful in art.

When they first started to worship the Hindu Prince Gautama, they began to make images for his temples, to arrange flowers on his altars, and to paint pictures for his shrines. The bells of the Buddhist temples rang softly in the morning and in the evening, and inspired the artists of Japan to make beautiful decorations for their Hindu Prince. In that way the people of Japan learned to appreciate and love all things beautiful.

Through Confucianism the Japanese gained their love of learning.

From the Sage of China they learned that a good man always adds new knowledge to the old knowledge, and they followed his teachings closely. From him, too, they learned to admire self-control, to cultivate good manners, and to develop a sense of humor.

Just as the man who loves learning, might also love art, and might also love nature, so, in Japan, some of the people follow all three religions, Confucianism, Buddhism, and Shintoism, at one and the same time.

Though Shintoism is dearest to the Japanese because it is their own and their oldest religion, Buddhism has the greatest number of followers, and Confucianism has the greatest influence.

In Japan today, as in China today, we find the greatest influence on the lives and thoughts of the people coming from one who did not teach anything new, but gathered the teachings of his forefathers; who did not teach anything about God or Heaven, but taught how people ought to live on earth; and who in his own life was a great example and model for the Good Man.

Little did Shuh-liang Heih the Valiant dream that his child, Ch'iu, born in Lu, in the District of Tsow, would become the teacher of two great Empires!

ZEN BUDDHISM

There are many sects among the Buddhists. The Buddhists of Thailand and Ceylon are quite different from their brothers-in-faith in Japan and Mongolia. Those of the South follow *Hinayana,* whereas those of the North follow *Mahayana,* which is more complicated in its ritual and beliefs.

And both branches have many sects which, though there is no strife among them, differ greatly in their way of following the teachings of the Buddha.

There is one sect, found mainly in Japan and influenced greatly by Shinto, which is so different and lofty in its ritual and practices that it has attracted wide attention in the Western world. It is called *Zen Buddhism.* The Zen Buddhists differ not so much in what they believe as in how they practice their beliefs. Central in their ideas is the conviction that one cannot learn the truth about the world from Sacred Books, and that truth resides in every one of us; but to discover it, we must lead a contemplative life, live simply, not be overjoyed when successful nor too depressed when met by adversity. And, above all, we should strive to do all things with dignity and beauty.

The Zen Buddhists depend on intuition to guide them; and the enlightenment they seek is of an ineffable and therefore mystic nature. They are respected everywhere for carrying into practice what they profoundly believe, even though the explanation of their beliefs is conveyed through mystic riddles.

BOOK THREE

THE ADVANCE OF THE ONE GOD

Part One: ZOROASTRIANISM

SPARK OF THE SACRED FIRE

> *"I praise aloud the thought well thought, the word well spoken, and the deed well done."*
>
> PART OF A ZOROASTRIAN PRAYER

FOUNDED: 6th Century B.C.

FOUNDER: Zoroaster (which comes from the Greek Zarathustra), who lived between 660-583 B.C. or 570-500 B.C. The scholars disagree about the dates.

PLACE: Ancient Persia (now Iran)

SACRED BOOKS: The *Avestas,* which contain hymns, sections of liturgy, and codes of purity.

NUMBER OF ADHERENTS: There are only about 125,000 Zoroastrians (or Parsees) in the world.

DISTRIBUTION: A number of Zoroastrians are still to be found in Persia (Iran); but most of them live in India.

ZOROASTRIANISM:

Spark of the Sacred Fire

1. TIES OF THE SACRED GIRDLE

At the end of the day, in the city called Bombay, in the Empire of India, a number of tall and dignified men, dressed in white robes tied with woven girdles, make their way through the colorful crowds of the city to the beach on the Arabian Sea.

At the edge of the water on the beach they stop, dip their hands into the water, and raise them ceremoniously to their foreheads. Then they untie their girdles and raise them to their foreheads.

After tying the girdles on again about their robes they raise their solemn faces to the setting sun and whisper:

"Humata, Hakhata, Hvershta!"

These are words of a long forgotten tongue that mean:

"I praise aloud the thought well thought, the word well spoken, and the deed well done!"

If the weather is clear and the day is pleasant, the beach of Bombay at sunset is covered with white-robed men who have come to worship in the open, with the setting sun as their altar.

When the sun has set, and its last glow has turned purple in the darkening sky, they turn and bow three times to the west, and three times to the south, and three times to the east, and three times to the north. Then they dip their hands again into the dark waters of the sea, raise their hands to their foreheads, and the ceremony is over.

Even in India, land of so many diverse beliefs, these people and their ways seem strange.

These people are not Hindus, and they do not belong to any of the great number of sects of Hinduism. They are called Fire-Worshippers because in their temples they always keep a fire burning.

For Fire to them is sacred.

Yet not Fire alone is sacred to them. Water and the Earth, also, they consider as sacred and holy.

When a Fire-Worshipper dies, they cannot cremate his

body, as the Hindus do, for fear of making the Sacred
Fire unclean.

They cannot throw the body into the waters of the sea,
for fear of making the Sacred Water unclean.

And they cannot bury the body in the ground for fear
of making the Sacred Earth unclean.

They place the bodies of their dead on top of high
towers that are built like huge chimneys. These towers
they call:

The Towers of Silence.

These people have many other strange ways and customs. But the Fire they keep always burning in their temples, and their Towers of Silence mark them as being different from all the other creeds in India, as well as any
other creed in the world.

These people are known as *Parsees,* which means:
Persians. Though they have lived in India for hundreds of
years, they are still called Parsees (Persians), foreigners
from a foreign land who follow the path of their forefathers, tied with the Sacred Girdle to the teachings and
memory of Zoroaster, the Prophet of the Wise Lord, who
lived many centuries ago in the land of Iran, that is now
known as Persia.

2. IN THE LAND OF IRAN LONG AGO

Northwest of India, close to the Caspian Sea, there lived
many, many centuries ago a people called Iranians in a
land called Iran.

From what we know now, the Iranians were very much
like the people who invaded India and who later wrote
the *Vedas.* They talked a language much like that of India
nearly 4000 years ago. They believed in many gods like
the gods of India at that time. And they worshipped the
cow, as the Hindus did.

But the Hindus were in India, and the Iranians were in
Iran. And the climate and conditions in the two countries
were not the same.

Being much farther to the north, it was colder in Iran.
And where the climate is much colder people must have
more clothes to wear, richer food to eat, and warmer
houses to live in. And in order to get more clothes, richer
food, and warmer houses, they must work much harder
and longer than people in a warm climate.

Iran was also a place where savage tribes from the Arabian deserts and the Caucasian plains swooped down upon the land, robbed the people of their cattle, and plundered their crops.

The life of the Iranian shepherd and farmer was not an easy life to lead. His southern Hindu neighbor lived a peaceful life, but the life of the Iranian was full of hardships, fear, and danger.

When people are hungry and troubled they are apt to think less of life after death than of bread and peace. And so when the Iranians prayed to their many gods, they prayed not for *Nirvana* as did the Hindus, but for the crops to be plentiful and for victory over their enemies.

Living always in fear of nomad tribes, the Iranians began to look upon every man who did not do some useful work as an evil person.

Only the tillers of the soil and the herders of the sheep and cattle were respected and considered good.

In India there were thousands upon thousands of monks who lived on charity, and yet they were highly respected by the people. But in Iran any man who did not work for his livelihood was looked down upon and distrusted.

Their struggle for existence was hard. Their methods of irrigating and cultivating the land were very primitive. And whatever crop they succeeded in raising they raised with much trouble and labor. Naturally they hated anyone who expected to share the fruits of their labor with them without himself doing anything in return.

Like all farmers of long, long ago, the Iranians worshipped many Nature-gods. They worshipped the Sun-god that ripened their crops; they worshipped the Rain-god that watered their fields; they worshipped the Cloud-god, and the Wind-god, and all the other Nature-gods that helped them in their work. These helpful Nature-gods they called *Daivas,* Good Spirits.

When the winter ended and spring began, and it was seeding-time on the land, the Iranians would go up to the mountains and pray to their Nature-gods to help them raise a good crop that year. And when the summer ended and the crops were gathered, the Iranians would go up to the mountain-tops again, worship and praise the Nature-gods and make sacrifices of fruit and grain and young lambs.

That was a very simple religion.

But it did not remain simple very long. For the people of Iran began to believe not only in the *Daivas,* the Good Spirits of Nature, but also in Clan-gods, Family-gods, and many other kinds of gods and spirits.

With the multiplication of their gods, images and idols made their appearance. They chiselled them out of stone, they moulded them out of clay, and they painted them on panels of wood. The rich people made their idols of gold and silver.

The Iranians no longer went out into the fields or up into the mountains to worship their gods. With the appearance of idols in Iran, Temples were built to them. And there the people gathered to offer up sacrifices and prayers.

Gradually the prayers, hymns and sacrifices to the different gods increased. The people who were busy tilling the soil and looking after their flocks, and protecting their property against the nomad tribes and their enemies, could not remember all the hymns that had to be sung to the different gods; nor could they remember which prayers ought to be murmured at what time; and they did not know what was the proper sacrifice to make to one god that would not make the other gods angry or jealous.

So they employed certain men who had learned just exactly how to make the sacrifices and when to sing the right hymns to the right god. These people who looked after the idols in the temples were called Priests.

Because the priests were always in the company of the gods they began to believe that they were better than all the other people in Iran. They also claimed that they knew how to please the *Daivas,* the Good Spirits, and in that way make the gods do whatever they (the priests) wished.

The Iranians believed their priests. They looked upon them as intermediaries between the gods and the people. Whenever the Iranians went to war they took their priests and favorite idols along to help them win their battles.

The priests who claimed that they could influence the idols and control the outcome of wars were called *Magi.* And the methods they used in influencing the gods were called *Magic.*

If the Magi can influence the gods to win their wars for them, so the people thought, surely they can even more easily influence the gods to make their cows give more milk, make their fields bear better crops, and grow more wool upon their sheep.

The Magi said that if they only wished to they could do all those things, and much more.

The belief in the power of the Magi spread among the people. And Idol-worship and sorcery and the belief in magic became worse and worse in the land of Iran.

3. THE CHILDHOOD OF A GREAT PROPHET

In the town called Azerbaijan, west of the Caspian Sea, there lived a man named Porushasp Spitama, of the Spitama Clan, and his beautiful wife Dughdova.

In the year 660 B.C., nearly 2600 years ago, Dughdova gave birth to a son who was named Zarathustra, whom we call Zoroaster.

There are many stories told about what happened before, and immediately after, Zoroaster's birth.

One story tells that when Zoroaster was born, Durasan, the Chief-Magician of Iran, began to tremble in great fear. For he knew a child was born who would grow up to destroy magic and Idol-worship, and who would banish all Magicians from the land.

Durasan sent three of his magicians to bring the child Zoroaster to him in the Fire-Temple. Meanwhile Durasan had prepared a great fire on the altar. When the baby was brought to him he placed him in the center of the fire, and he and his magicians left the temple.

That, thought Durasan, would be the end of Zoroaster. But he was mistaken.

When Zoroaster's mother came home and found her baby gone, she ran to the Fire-Temple to pray. And there, on the altar, she found her child playing happily in the midst of the flames as if he were splashing about in a lukewarm bath.

Durasan was now certain that Zoroaster was no ordinary child, and he fell upon a new plan. He called his three magicians and ordered them again to get the child Zoroaster and place him in the middle of a highway where a large herd of cattle was to pass.

But the first cow of the herd ran up to the child, stepped over him in a manner to protect him from the others, and stood there until the entire herd had passed. When Zoroaster's mother came running up the road in search of her child she found him upon the ground unhurt.

The Chief-Magician was more frightened than ever. For three days and three nights he sat planning and planning. Then he decided upon a new plan. This time the child Zoroaster was to be stolen and placed in a wolves' den.

"Even if the wolves do not kill him," thought Durasan, "the child will die of hunger."

When the hungry wolves came home they sniffed the air, aware that someone was in their den. But as soon as they tried to come near they became fixed to the ground and could not move.

Meanwhile little Zoroaster became very hungry and began to cry. Immediately two goats appeared, walked right into the wolves' den, and fed the baby.

Of course, those were not ordinary goats, so the story tells, but were really angels in disguise.

This is only one of many, many stories told about what happened to the child Zoroaster when he was still very small.

Naturally his father and mother expected their son to grow up to be a great man.

"We must give our son a good education," said the father.

"The best in the land," said the mother.

When Zoroaster was seven years old he was sent away to study with Burzin-kurus who was known all over Iran for his wisdom. For eight years Zoroaster remained with the wise Burzin-kurus studying not only religion, but also farming, cattle-raising, and healing.

At the end of that time Zoroaster returned home and put on the Sacred Shirt and the Sacred Girdle which, like the putting on of the Sacred Thread by the Hindus, was a symbol of his being confirmed into the religion of his people.

4. ZOROASTER IN SEARCH OF TRUTH

Soon after Zoroaster returned home, Iran was invaded by the Turanians of the neighboring country. Young Zoroaster immediately volunteered to go out into the battle fields and apply his knowledge of healing to the wounded soldiers.

At the close of the war a famine broke out all over Iran and the sickness and need in the land was as great as during the war. Again Zoroaster volunteered to work amongst the sick and the poor.

For five years young Zoroaster devoted himself to his noble work. Then he returned home. His father wanted his son to give up his work amongst the people, get married, and settle down to the life of a respectable land-owner and cattle-raiser.

Zoroaster followed his father's advice as far as marrying a beautiful girl named Havovee. But he would not settle down to the life of a farmer. His experiences on the battle field, and during the famine, convinced him that he was destined to more important work than growing grain or raising cattle. And he went on with his work amongst the sick of the land.

For ten more years Zoroaster was active amongst the poor and the needy, his mind constantly planning methods to alleviate the suffering of his people. But their sorrows and misfortunes seemed to have no end.

Zoroaster began to wonder where all the evil in the world came from.

If he only knew the source of suffering, he thought, his dream of making all his people happy and strong would come true.

"Havovee," Zoroaster said to his wife one day, "I am going away to live like a hermit for a while and think of good and evil. Perhaps I can discover the source of suffering in the world."

His wife thought it foolish of him to waste his time in search of the sources of good and evil, when he might be raising cattle and growing rich.

But Zoroaster left his home and went up to Mount Sabalan, determined not to return home until he had gained the wisdom he was seeking.

For days and weeks and months Zoroaster remained alone thinking and thinking, and trying to understand the world.

He thought of all he had learned from his wise teacher, Burzin-kurus.

He thought of all he had learned from his father and the priests.

And he thought of all his experiences amongst the people during the war and the famine and the years that followed.

But in none of these could he find any explanation of the world of good and evil.

One day Zoroaster sat in front of his cave on the mountain side. He wondered whether he ought not to give up his search for the source of suffering and return to his wife and children.

The sun began to sink beyond the horizon and the sky in front of Zoroaster turned golden and red and purple. Slowly the glowing sun sank beyond the row of hills, and darkness began to flood the valley below.

Suddenly Zoroaster jumped to his feet aglow with joy.

He had the beginning of the wisdom he was seeking!

The realization came to him as he had watched the sunset that the day is divided into day and night—light and darkness!

This ordinary fact had been known to him since childhood. But in it Zoroaster had now discovered the Key to Wisdom.

Just as every day consists of light and darkness, Zoroaster thought, so the world consists of Good and Evil.

Just as the day and the night can never change their nature and must always be the same, the day being bright and the night being dark, so Good can never become Evil, and Evil can never become Good.

The Good must always be good, and the Evil must always be evil.

If good is always good, and evil always evil, Zoroaster thought, then the Magicians and Idol-worshipping Priests who believe that one can pray to the good gods to do evil to their enemies, or to the evil gods to do good, must be wrong.

The good gods can never do evil, and the evil gods can never do good.

It was very clear to Zoroaster that the world was ruled by two forces: One Good, and One Evil. The Good Force of the world Zoroaster named *Ahura Mazda.* And the Evil Force he named *Angra Manyu.*

Though Zoroaster had the Key to Wisdom, it was still not very clear to him why Good and Evil were created, or how people ought to live to do away with evil and suffering.

He remained on Mount Sabalan, slowly clarifying his thoughts, slowly advancing from his discovery that good is always good and evil always evil to an understanding of how people ought to live in order to be good.

"Now," Zoroaster said to himself, "now I shall go down

and lead my people from darkness into light, from suffering to happiness, and from Evil to Good!"

5.   IN THE PALACE OF KING VISHTASPA

Zoroaster came from Mount Sabalan enthusiastically ready to proclaim to the people the truth about Good and Evil. But the people of Iran were not as ready to listen to him.

The people of Iran were accustomed to gods and idols that were actual to them. But the God of Good and the Spirit of Evil that Zoroaster preached were not to be seen, nor to be heard, nor to be touched. And whatever the people of that day could not see with their eyes, or touch with their hands, or hear with their ears, that they would not believe.

Not even Zoroaster's family would believe in his teachings.

For ten long years he went about in search of believers. And in all that time he won over only one follower, his own cousin.

Zoroaster was already forty years old and his hair was greying at his temples.

"Your teachings are too hard for people to understand," said Zoroaster's cousin.

"Yes," Zoroaster reflected sadly.

"If you could get the attention of the educated people who are trained to understand difficult thoughts and ideas, then you'd get a hearing."

"You are right," said Zoroaster.

And who were the most learned in the land if not the King and the Queen and the rest of the Royal family?

To them Zoroaster decided to go and explain his new religion. He immediately started out for Bactria where lived King Kavi Vishtaspa, in the city of Balkh.

With the dust of the long journey still upon his shoes, Zoroaster appeared at the gates of the Royal Palace, and said to the Guardian of the Gates:

"Go, and tell King Vishtaspa that I, Zoroaster Spitama, Prophet of the One Wise Lord, have come to see him and to teach him the ways of Good and Evil!"

The Guardian of the Gates thought that Zoroaster was an impudent beggar, and he burst into laughter.

"Go, and do as I bid you do!" Zoroaster commanded.

The Guardian of the Gates stopped laughing, for there

was something in Zoroaster's commanding voice and in his fiery eyes that frightened him. But he still did not move from his post.

Zoroaster then took out a ball of fire, so one story tells, and held it in his outstretched hand.

"Let this be a sign to you that I come in the name of the One Wise Lord!" Zoroaster said.

The Guardian of the Gates ran at once to the throne-room where the King sat on his throne surrounded by his Wise Men, Priests and Magicians.

"A truly marvelous man has come wishing to see you, Your Majesty! He claims to be the Prophet of the One Wise Lord, and in his hand he holds a ball of fire that burns, yet does not burn his hand!"

"Send him in!" the King commanded.

Zoroaster walked into the throne-room and said in a firm voice:

"I, Zoroaster Spitama, Prophet of the One Wise Lord, have come to you, Mighty King, to turn your heart from vain and evil idols towards the glory of the True and Wise and Eternal Lord!"

"What sign have you to offer that your words are true?" the King asked.

"I teach the word of Truth against the word of False-hood. If you or your wise men wish to question me, I shall answer and prove your ways of Idol-worship to be wrong and shadowed with the darkness of night; and the way of the One Wise Lord, *Ahura Mazda,* to be good and bright as the light of day."

"Wise Men, Priests, and Magicians!" the King addressed his men, "question this stranger on his teachings, and I shall sit in judgment and decide who is right and who is wrong!"

"If you find my words to be true," said Zoroaster to the King, "promise that you will abandon the dark ways of Idol-worship and follow the shining road of the Wise Lord!"

"I promise!" said the King.

Then the debate between Zoroaster and the King's Wise Men, Priests and Magicians began.

6. THE DEBATE THAT LASTED THREE DAYS

"What is this new religion that you teach, and how is it different from the religion of your forefathers?" the Chief Priest asked Zoroaster angrily.

"I have come not to teach a new religion, but to improve the old," Zoroaster replied. "What I teach is the Truth of the Creator, and therefore good. Your Idol-worship is not true, and therefore it is evil."

"Do you mean that our gods, the Sun, the Fire, the Mountains, and the Stars are false gods?" the Chief Priest asked.

"No," Zoroaster replied, "they are not false gods. They are not gods at all. If a man makes a house, would you call the house the man? Even so the sun, moon and mountains are not gods, but the works of the Creator?"

"Who is that Creator?" one of the magicians asked.

"*Ahura Mazda,* Lord of Wisdom, Supreme Ruler of the World!" Zoroaster replied.

"And you say that he created everything in the world?" one of the Wise Men asked.

"He created everything that is good in the world. For God is Good."

"And who created the evil of the world?"

"*Angra Manyu,* the Evil Spirit, created all that is evil in the world."

"Then there is more than one god in the world!" the Chief Priest shouted triumphantly.

"Yes," Zoroaster replied. "There are two Creators. In the beginning there were two spirits: one Good and one Evil. And the Good Spirit said to the Evil Spirit, 'Your ways are not my ways, your thoughts are not my thoughts, your words are not my words, and your deeds are not my deeds. Let us separate!' Then the Good Spirit created all the good in the world, and the Evil Spirit made all the evil in the world."

"Then why do you say we should follow the Good Spirit? Why not follow the Evil Spirit who is just as great as the Good Spirit?" the wise man asked again.

"Because Good will win over Evil in the end."

"How do you know that?" a magician asked.

"Because *Evil has no foresight!*" Zoroaster replied slowly.

And after a pause, he explained:

"The Wise Lord remembers the past and understands the future. But the Evil Spirit does not know the past nor the future. Evil lives only for the profits of the present. That is why the Wise One will win the battle over Evil in the end."

"And who created Man?" a wise man asked.

"*Ahura Mazda,* the Wise Lord, created Man," Zoroaster replied.

"You said that the Good Spirit can do only good and create only good things. Then how is it that Man, created by the Good Spirit, is following the ways of the Evil Spirit?"

"That is because Man was created with a free will to choose between good and evil," Zoroaster replied. "But all the thoughts a man thinks and all the words a man speaks and all the deeds a man does each day of his life are written down in the Book of Life. The good thoughts, words and deeds are written down on one side, and the bad thoughts, words and deeds are written down on the other side. When a man dies his soul comes up to the Keeper of the Book of Life. If his good thoughts, words and deeds are greater than his evil thoughts, words and deeds, then the soul goes to Heaven. Otherwise the soul must go down to the tortures of Hell."

"And will this go on forever?" the King asked.

"No, Your Majesty!" Zoroaster replied. "For the Day of Judgment is nigh. And on that Day of Days the Wise Lord will triumph over the Evil Spirit. Good will triumph over Evil. Then all the dead will come to life again. The good souls and the bad souls will be tried. They will pass through a flow of molten metal. To the good it will seem like passing through warm milk. But the evil will burn everlastingly. And then the Good Lord will banish the Evil Spirit and all the evil souls into the middle of the earth and keep them there forever. And on that Day of Days the good and happy world without evil will begin and last forever!"

All the men in the throne-room were silent, for they had never heard such strange words before. And the King asked his men:

"Have you no other questions to ask this man?"

"What ought one to do to follow the ways of the Wise Lord?" one wise man immediately asked Zoroaster.

"*Humata, Hakhata, Hvarshta!* Good thoughts, good words, and good deeds! This is the Way to the Wise Lord!"

"How is one to know which thoughts, words and deeds are good?"

"That is easy to tell: *Truth is good; falsehood is evil!*" Zoroaster replied.

"Is Truth alone the way to the Wise Lord?"

"*Truth* comes first," answered Zoroaster. "But there are others. The follower of the Way of the Wise Lord must be

"*Pure* in thoughts, words and deeds, he must be

"*Charitable* and help all in need; he must

"*Work the land*, grow trees, raise cattle or do other profitable and useful labor; and he must be

"*Kind* to all useful animals."

Then Zoroaster explained that the reward for the good deeds is not only in the life to come, but even here on earth. And he gave a full list of all the good deeds and their rewards; and all the evil deeds, and their punishment.

For three days and three nights the king's men kept asking questions. And Zoroaster answered them all.

The King who had sat listening attentively exclaimed:

"Surely this man, who can speak so wisely and banish you all in argument is the Prophet of the Wise Lord!"

7. THE TRIUMPH OF ZOROASTER

The King kept his promise and accepted the teachings of the One Wise Lord. He proclaimed Zoroaster as the True Prophet of this new religion, and made him High Priest in the Royal Palace.

The news of the King's conversion became known through Iran, and many people accepted Zoroaster's teachings. His family, who had refused to listen to him for over ten years, came and paid homage to him.

Zoroaster was very happy. At last he had won a victory over the Idol-worshippers and the magicians, and found followers willing to accept his teachings.

But his happiness did not last long.

The Court Magicians and the Idol-worshipping Priests gathered in secrecy to plot against Zoroaster.

"If this man wins the confidence of the King," they said, "then our days are at an end."

They wished they could kill Zoroaster. But they knew that if the King found out who had done it he would have them all beheaded.

"I have a plan!" whispered one Magician.

"What is it?"

"The King hates sorcerers and conjurers—"

"Yes, yes—"

"Then let us accuse this man Zoroaster of being a sorcerer."

"But how will you prove it?"

"That is easy," said the Magician. "When Zoroaster leaves his room, we will hide in it everything necessary to convict him."

"Wisely spoken!" all the others agreed.

The next day they went to the King and said:

"This man Zoroaster, who calls himself the Prophet of the One Wise Lord, is only a conjurer and a sorcerer of evil. And if you have his room searched you will find that our words are true."

The King immediately sent messengers to search Zoroaster's room. When they returned with cats' and dogs' heads, bones of every kind, nails and hair and all the other things that sorcerers used in those days, the King ordered Zoroaster arrested and put into prison.

Just then the King's favorite horse took sick and could not rise upon its feet.

All the Court Magicians gathered in the stables to bring the horse back to health by magic.

All the Royal Priests gathered in the stables to pray the steed back to his strength.

All the King's Physicians came to the stables and rubbed the steed's legs with oils and ointments.

But the magic, and the ointments, and the prayers of the Priests were of no avail. The King's favorite horse lay upon the floor of the Royal Stables, its legs withered like dry twigs.

Zoroaster, who had heard what had happened, sent word from the prison saying that he could bring the horse back to health. His message created a stir in the Palace, and he was at once brought to the Royal Stables, where the entire Royal Family, and the Court Magicians, and the King's Physicians, and the Idol-worshipping Priests had gathered to see what Zoroaster could do.

"If I restore your horse to health," Zoroaster addressed the King, "do you promise that you will accept my teachings and never forsake them?"

"I promise!" said the King.

Zoroaster rubbed one of the horse's withered legs, and it immediately became well. Zoroaster stopped in his work and again addressed the King:

"If I restore your horse to health, do you promise that your son, the Prince, will accept my teachings?"

"I promise!" said the King.

Zoroaster rubbed a second of the horse's withered legs, and that, too, immediately became well.

"If I restore your horse to health," Zoroaster asked again, "do you promise that your Queen, too, will accept my teachings?"

"I promise!" said the King.

Zoroaster rubbed the third leg of the sick horse, and that, too, became well again.

Zoroaster looked sternly about him at all the people who were watching him in admiration and awe.

"Do you promise," he said to the King, "that you will punish those who plotted against me and accused me falsely of sorcery?"

"I promise!" said the King.

Zoroaster rubbed the fourth leg of the sick horse, and it jumped up to its feet, well again.

The King immediately sent out an order that 12,000 cows be killed, and the 12,000 hides be tanned, and the hides be bound with rings of pure gold. And on these hides he ordered the scribes to write down in letters of gold the teachings of Zoroaster, Prophet of the One Wise Lord.

The teachings of Zoroaster were called ZORO-ASTRIANISM.

And the book into which his teachings were written down was called THE AVESTA.

The *Avesta* became the Sacred Scriptures of Zoro-astrianism.

And Zoroaster Spitama was made High Priest to King Kavi Vishtaspa in the Court of Balkh, in the Land of Iran.

8.   THE HOLY WARS

Zoroaster had a daughter called Porucista, and she was famed as the wisest woman in the Kingdom.

Porucista came to the Royal Palace to see her father who had been appointed High Priest in the Court of Balkh. Her wisdom soon gained the admiration of the entire Royal Family. And the Prime Minister of Balkh asked her to be his wife.

There was only one Prime Minister in the whole of

Balkh, and Porucista, being a very wise woman, did not refuse him.

With the Prime Minister as his son-in-law, Zoroaster's position in the Court was, naturally, well established.

One day Zoroaster said to King Vishtaspa:

"Your Majesty, if it is true that *Ahura Mazda,* the Wise Lord, created *all* that was good in the entire world, and that the Evil Spirit created *all* the evil in the world, then surely their kingdoms are not only Iran, but the entire world."

"That seems true," said the King.

"If it is true, then the teachings about the One Wise Lord were meant for *all* men, everywhere!"

"That, too, sounds true!" said the King.

"If it is true that the teachings of the Wise Lord are meant for all of Mankind, then it is our duty to spread our teachings everywhere," said Zoroaster.

The King agreed with him and ordered missionaries to go out and teach the *Avesta* all over Iran, and outside of Iran in all the neighboring Kingdoms.

Soon the teachings of the *Avesta* became known all over Iran. They passed into Turan. And even in Greece, and even in India these teachings became known. But the number of followers of Zoroaster's teachings outside of Iran were not many in number.

When Zoroaster was sixty years old he decided to force the neighboring people of Turan to accept Zoroastrianism.

The Iranians were in debt to the Kingdom of Turan, and Zoroaster asked King Vishtaspa to send the following message to Turan:

"If you, King of Turan, and your people, will not give up your evil ways of Idol-worship, and accept the teachings of the Wise Lord as written down in the *Avesta* and as preached by the Prophet Zoroaster Spitama, then we will refuse to pay our debt to you!"

This message made the King of Turan very angry. He called together his Wise Men and asked them what to do.

"If in the name of religion they can refuse to pay their debts," said one of the Wise Men, "then in the name of the same religion they may also wish to take away our land and our freedom."

They all agreed upon sending to Iran the following reply:

"I, King of Turan, and my people, send you this warning:

Unless you give up the teachings of Zoroaster and return to the faith of your forefathers, we shall be down upon you with our armies and our spears before the end of three moons!"

And so war broke out between Iran and Turan over the religion of Zoroaster, Prophet of the One Wise Lord.

After many fierce battles the Iranians won great victories over Turan. Zoroaster, who had caused the war, became the great hero of his people. His words were law, and his teachings sacred. And the people worshipped him.

That was in Iran.

In Turan they hated him and planned revenge. For seventeen years they plotted against Zoroaster and the Iranians. And when they felt strong enough to go to war again, the Turanians attacked the Kingdom of Iran. Shortly afterwards they besieged the city of Balkh and captured it.

At the time the walls of the city fell before the enemy, Zoroaster was in a temple praying for the victory of his people in the Holy War which he had started. As he knelt before the Sacred Fire, a Turanian soldier rushed into the temple and stabbed the old prophet in the back.

So died Zoroaster, Prophet of the One Wise Lord.

9. THE FIRE THAT ALWAYS BURNS

King Vishtaspa made a vow to avenge the death of the slain prophet. He organized all his forces and renewed his attacks upon the Turanians until they were defeated. Not until they promised to accept Zoroastrianism as their religion did King Vishtaspa make peace with his neighbors.

As soon as the war was over the King sent out missionaries to other lands to spread the teachings of Zoroastrianism.

With time the teachings of Zoroaster slowly changed.

When Zoroaster had been asked whether the Wise Lord was alone in his work of Good in the world, he answered that the Wise Lord had Heavenly Assistants, called Angels, to do his bidding. The most important of these Angels, he said, were six:

> Good Mind
> Good Order
> Wisdom
> Piety
> Well-being
> Immortality

From the names of these Angels we can easily understand that Zoroaster did not mean that the Angels of the Wise Lord were actual angels with wings, harps and haloes as we sometimes see in pictures. What Zoroaster meant was that these were the various *characteristics* of the Wise Lord.

Just as, for instance, we say that Abraham Lincoln had a love of justice, that he had wisdom, that he had a good mind, that he had a love for his country and his people. By that we do not mean that he had these things in his trunk or that they were servants in his house. What we mean is that they were part of his character: they were his *characteristics*.

In the same way Zoroaster meant that Good Mind, Good Order, Wisdom, Piety, Well-being, and Immortality were *characteristics* of the Wise Lord of the World.

But the Priests and the people of Iran had been Idol-worshippers. Though they accepted the teachings of Zoroaster, they still had the minds of Idol-worshippers. When Zoroaster told them about the characteristics of the Wise Lord, they imagined them as real angels that flew about like a flock of white birds, blowing golden horns, and singing Hymns.

Before very long they named thousands of white angels who lived in Heaven above, and 99,999 black demons who helped the Evil Spirit in the hell below.

In that way they did just what Zoroaster did not want them to do: they worshipped the old idols, only they gave them new names.

Zoroaster also believed that the world would come to an end in his own day. But after his death the Zoroastrian Priests told their followers that the Wise Lord created the world in Six Periods, of two months each, and that the world would last a thousand years for each month of Creation.

Zoroaster, they said, was born at the end of nine thousand years after Creation. And three thousand years after his death a son of Zoroaster would appear on earth. This Son of Zoroaster will be the *Sayoshant,* the Messiah, the Savior of Mankind.

The beliefs and teachings of Zoroaster were changed by his followers.

But the most important teachings of the Prophet of the One Wise Lord remain at the foundation of their religion to this day.

Zoroaster was the first religious leader in the world to teach the belief in an abstract god, a god one could not touch or hear or smell or see. That god was *Ahura Mazda,* the One Wise Lord who created all that was good in the world and whom we know only through his works.

Zoroaster also taught that when a man does good, not only is the deed recorded in the Book of Life and the doer rewarded, but the Doer of Good also adds to the Good of the World.

Therefore, Zoroaster preached, it is the duty of Man to do good not only for the reward one gets, but also because, in doing good, people add to the Good of the World and help *Ahura Mazda* win his battle with *Angra Manyu,* the Evil Spirit.

The Doer of Evil is in league with the Evil Spirit. But the Doer of Good fights the Battles of the Wise Lord.

Zoroaster urged his followers to fight the Battles of the Lord through:

Purity of thought, word and deed;

Cleanliness;

Charity of heart;

Kindliness to useful animals;

Doing profitable work; and

Helping people, who cannot afford it, to receive a good education.

They who follow these teachings can be said to be followers in the Ways of the One Wise Lord.

10.   ZOROASTRIANISM TODAY

Nearly three hundred years after Zoroaster died, Alexander the Great, King of Macedonia, conquered Persia. He destroyed the *Avesta,* it is told, and in the place of Zoroastrianism set up the religion of the Greeks of that day.

But the people of Persia did not wish to give up their religion, and secretly taught it to their children.

When the Persians became independent of foreign rule, about five hundred years later, they restored the teachings of Zoroaster. They gathered into books the parts of the old *Avesta* that had been saved and remembered by the people.

Much of the old *Avesta* was lost. But the newly gathered *Avesta* began to spread over Persia, and new Fire Temples were built. In these temples a fire was kept burning all the time as a symbol of the One Wise Lord who lives forever.

About four hundred years later the Arabs conquered Persia. And with them they brought a new religion which they forced upon the people at the point of the sword. Anyone who refused to accept their religion was put to death.

There were many in Iran who would rather die than accept a new religion they did not believe in.

There were some who accepted the new religion, rather than die.

And others ran away to lands where they were permitted to practise their religion as they pleased.

Today there are few Zoroastrians left in Persia. Most of the Zoroastrians live in India, the country they ran away to over 1300 years ago.

Though these Zoroastrians, called *Parsees,* believed and believe that their religion is the best in the world, they did not and do not teach it to the Hindus. Not only that, they even prohibit anyone from becoming a Zoroastrian who is not one by birth.

The *Parsees* realized that the best and most educated Hindus, who belonged to the High Castes, would not give up Hinduism and join any other religion. The only Hindus who would join a new religion would be the Outcasts who would try to find in a new religion teachings that would make them feel just as good as their superiors. And the *Parsees* realized that if they permitted the most ignorant people of India to join their religion, Zoroastrianism might soon sink to Idol-worship. And they decided that it was better to have just a few followers worthy of the Faith, rather than have many unworthy.

Today there are only about 100,000 Zoroastrians in the world. Yet this religion, small as it is in the number of its followers, is very important for its influence on other religions—as we shall soon see.

Part Two: JUDAISM

RELIGION OF MANY PROPHETS

"Lovers of Jehovah, hate evil!"
PSALM 97

FOUNDED: 13th Century B.C.

FOUNDER: Moses the son of Amram, who emancipated the Jews from Egyptian bondage and established a covenant between the people and Jehovah at Mount Sinai. (According to tradition, Abraham and his descendants established Judaism before Moses; but the Ten Commandments is now considered the foundation stone of Judaism.)

PLACE: Palestine or Canaan (now Israel).

SACRED BOOKS: *The Old Testament,* which consists of the Five Books of Law, the historical books, the Prophets, and other miscellaneous writings. The books held most sacred are the Five Books of the Law, called the *Torah.*

NUMBER OF ADHERENTS: About 11,500,000

DISTRIBUTION: Jews are to be found in small numbers the world over. About two million live in Asia, mostly in Israel; three and a half million live in Europe, most of them in Russia and Poland; and about six and a half million are in North and South America, most of them in the United States.

JEWS IN THE UNITED STATES: About five million

SECTS: Jews are divided into: Orthodox, Conservative and Reform. Within each category there are sects and divisions.

JUDAISM:

Religion of Many Prophets

1. THE SCATTERED PEOPLE

There are many millions of people in the world today. And amongst them, everywhere, is scattered a nation known as the Children of Israel, called Jews.

Far to the east and far to the west they are to be found. And as far north as north can go, and as far south as south can go, almost wherever there are people, there are Jews.

There are a few Jews in Abyssinia as dark as any man in that land.

There are a few Jews in China who, like the Chinese, are yellow-skinned and their eyes are almond-shaped and slanted.

There are Jews in Italy, swarthy and black-eyed.

There are Jews in Northern Russia, Canada, Sweden and Norway with blonde hair, white skins, and greenish-grey eyes.

And there are Jews in Denmark, Germany and Ireland who are red-haired and blue-eyed.

There are short, dark-haired Jews in warmer climates.

There are tall, light-skinned Jews in colder countries.

There are the slender daughters of Zion in Palestine, and there are the fat Jewesses in Tunis and Morocco.

The Italian Jew speaks Italian. The English Jew speaks English. In Russia they speak Russian, and in China, Chinese. When these people of different lands meet they do not understand each other's language. Yet they do feel related to each other.

What makes these people kin to each other in spite of the difference in their physical appearance and the difference in the languages they speak?

There are many factors that bind these people together, scattered though they are, and the most important factor of all is their religion.

We have seen how the religion of Zoroaster keeps together his followers who have remained in a foreign country, India, for hundreds of years. And this is also true of

141

the Jews. For centuries they have lived, scattered over the earth, yet they have been held together and kept alive by their religion.

What is this strange religion that has had such hold upon the minds of this small and scattered race? How did it arise? Where did it grow? And what did it teach?

2. OVER FOUR THOUSAND YEARS AGO

The story of the Jewish Religion is the story of the Jewish People. And it began long ago:

In the city of Ur, in the land of the Chaldees, not far from where Zoroaster was born, there lived over 4000 years ago a man named Terah.

Terah, like the rest of his people, the Chaldeans, was an Idol-worshipper. In a land where people wear hats, hats are made. And in a land where people worship idols, idols are made. And Terah, son of Nahor, was an idol maker. He made them out of clay and stone, then sold them to the people of the land.

Terah had three sons, Abraham, Nahor, and Haran. Abraham and his brothers, it is believed, were shepherds in the green pasturelands of the Euphrates Valley. But sometimes they helped their old father with the making of the idols.

To worship idols that other people have made is one thing. To worship idols that one has fashioned oneself out of rough stone or wet clay is quite another matter. And to Abraham, who had much time for thought when he was out in the pastures with his sheep, it seemed strange to kneel and pray in the evening before a little image of a fox that he himself had made in the morning.

What strength and what power and what holiness was there in those idols of clay? Abraham wondered. And he could find no answer to this question. Instead of an answer, other questions came to his mind. And he did not dare ask his father or the priests of Ur, because to doubt the holiness of the idols was considered a great crime in Chaldea.

One day, when Abraham was left alone in his father's shop, he took an axe and smashed all the idols but one. And into the hands of the one he did not break he placed the axe. Then Abraham sat down to see what would happen.

A little later old Terah arrived. When he saw his ruined stock of idols he became very angry.

"Why did you break all our idols?" he demanded of his son.

"I did not do it, Father," Abraham replied. "That idol over there had a quarrel with the others and in a rage he took the axe and destroyed them all, as you see."

"That is not true!" Terah shouted. "You know that these idols cannot quarrel, nor fight, nor move! It was YOU who did it!"

"If it is true, as you say, that these idols cannot do anything, then what are they good for?" Abraham asked.

Terah had never heard such a question asked about the idols before, and he did not know what to answer.

"Why—they are—they are—they are to be worshipped—" Terah muttered.

"They have eyes but cannot see, they have ears but cannot hear, they have hands but cannot move," Abraham said. "Then surely they are good for nothing. And that is why I broke them, father! *Idols should not be worshipped!*"

"What then should people worship?" Terah, who had been an Idol-worshipper all his life, asked his son.

"Worship the gods that made the sun and the moon and the stars; worship the gods that bring each season in season, and that give us rain, and that make the fields rich with pasture, and the sheep heavy with lambs."

These were strange words for the son of an Idol-worshipper to dare say in those days. When it became known in Ur what Terah's oldest son did to his father's idols and what he had said about them it was no longer safe for Abraham and his family to remain in that land.

So Abraham and his wife and some of his relatives and their male servants and their female servants and their flocks of sheep and cattle and all they possessed left their birthplace, and wandered north towards the land called Canaan.

The people of Canaan called Abraham *Ibri* (Hebrew), meaning: From across—the man who came across the Euphrates and the Tigris.

And his family were also called *Ibris* (Hebrews).

These Hebrews differed from the rest of the Canaanites and Moabites and Amalikites and the Amorites and all the tribes that lived far and near in those lands. They did not differ so much in their speech or in their appearance. But they differed from the rest of the people in that all the other tribes worshipped idols, but the Hebrews were followers of the teachings of Abraham, believing, as they did, that *idols should not be worshipped*.

3. THE RISE OF THE CHILDREN OF ISRAEL

Abraham, the Idol-breaker, had a son called Isaac. Isaac had a son called Jacob. Jacob the son of Isaac was also called Israel. And his children were called the Children of Israel, or Israelites.

Jacob, called Israel, had twelve sons. These twelve sons had many children. And their children had many children.

Before very long the Israelites were a large and powerful tribe. They were herdsmen and wandered from place to place in search of good pastureland. The greater their tribe became, the easier it was for them to fight other tribes and to conquer the rich pasturelands they needed.

Once a great famine came upon the land of Canaan and all the lands around, and the Israelites decided to go down to Egypt where they had heard there was plenty of food and pasture for their flocks. When they came to Egypt, they were permitted to settle in the Province of Goshen, close to the Nile River.

For many years the Hebrews from Canaan and the Deserts of Shur lived happily in Goshen Land in Egypt. And their numbers grew from year to year. But they kept apart from the Egyptians and their temples and their religion.

The Egyptians, in so far as we know, had more idols than any other people living in those days. Their temples and palaces and homes were filled with idols of various kinds and sizes. They worshipped bulls and dogs, cats and crocodiles, fish and birds and beetles. Naturally they disliked these Hebrews who would not worship their idols.

They disliked them and also feared them. When the number of the Hebrews became great enough, the Egyptians feared, they might try to destroy the idols of Egypt.

The King called together his Priests and Magicians and Wise Men to ask them what to do about the Hebrews in their land before their number grew too great and their power too strong.

"Slaves do not think for themselves," the Wise Men

said. "Slaves think as their masters do. If the Hebrews were made slaves, they would think and believe as we do."

The King took their advice. And what the Wise Men said came true. When the Hebrews were made slaves, they slowly began to think the way the Egyptians did, and to worship the gods and idols the Egyptians worshipped.

Still they kept apart from the people of Egypt.

The King called his Priests, Magicians and Wise Men together again, and said to them:

"We have made slaves of the Hebrews, but still they keep apart and may be plotting against us. What shall we do now?"

"Let us pass a law," said the Wise Men, "that all the boys born to the Hebrews should be drowned. Then the girls of the Hebrews will have to marry Egyptians and become Egyptians like ourselves."

The suggestion pleased the King, and he had a law passed that all the Hebrew boys should be drowned as soon as they were born.

Just then a little Hebrew boy was born, who was named Moses. According to the new law he had to be drowned. But his mother could not drown her child. Yet she had to obey the law.

She put her child in a basket and let it float down the Nile.

But that is only the beginning of the story of Moses.

4. THE ROD IN JETHRO'S GARDEN

Moses was found by the King's daughter who came to bathe in the river that afternoon. The Princess took the baby home and adopted him as her own son.

But it seems that when Moses was old enough to understand he found out that he was a Hebrew. And when he grew older still he began to think of how to free his people from slavery.

One day Moses saw an Egyptian slave-driver cruelly beating two Hebrew slaves. In a rage, Moses killed the slave-driver.

He knew he was no longer safe in Egypt, and he ran away to the desert of Midian to hide.

In Midian, so one legend tells, Moses came into the garden of the Priest Jethro. Amongst the trees and shrubs in the garden Moses noticed a rod planted in the ground.

In appearance it was just an ordinary straight slender rod, round and smooth, such as the shepherds used.

"Why is that rod planted in your garden?" Moses asked Jethro.

"That rod? There is a story to that rod!" answered Jethro, and looked around over his garden. "When Joseph, son of Jacob, died in Egypt, all his belongings were taken to the King's treasure-house. Amongst the things Joseph left behind him was that rod. I was High Priest in King Pharaoh's Palace then, and when I saw the rod, I liked it. 'Could I have that rod?' I asked the King. And he said I could. Later, when I came out here to Midian, I accidentally stuck it into the ground. As soon as it was stuck into the ground it became so strongly rooted that no one could pull it out. All the strong men in Midian came and tried to pull it out and could not. And there it has been ever since."

"I wonder——" said Moses and narrowed his eyes as if trying to remember something.

"What do you wonder?" Jethro asked.

Moses looked at the head of the rod very carefully. On the very top were engraved the three Hebrew words:

Detzach, Adash, Vehachab

Above these three words was the Ineffable Name.

"Yes," said Moses to Jethro, "there *is* a story to that rod!"

"Another story?" Jethro asked.

"Yes, another story," said Moses. "At the end of the Sixth Day of Creation, just before the First Week ended and the First Sabbath began, God completed His Work by creating the Ten Wonders. One of the Ten Wonders was that very rod."

"That rod?" Jethro looked at it in great surprise.

"Yes," said Moses, "that rod! It was given to Adam the First when he was still in the Garden of Eden. Adam gave it to Enoch. Enoch gave it to Shem. Shem gave it to Abraham. Abraham gave it to Isaac. Isaac gave it to Jacob. When Jacob went down to Egypt he took that rod along with him and gave it to his son, Joseph. And there it is before you now."

Moses was a stranger in Midian, and Jethro thought he was one of those wandering Princes that tell marvelous tales.

"And how do I know that your words are true, Moses?" Jethro asked.

"You said that no one, not even the strongest man in Midian, could pull that rod out of the ground, didn't you?"

"Yes," replied Jethro.

Moses walked over to the rod and pulled it out as easily as if it were an ordinary cane stuck loosely into sand.

Then Jethro knew at once that Moses must be a very great man, and he gave him his daughter Zipporah as wife.

After his marriage Moses remained in his father-in-law's house, and helped Jethro look after his many flocks of sheep.

5.   OUT OF BONDAGE

Out on the hills, watching the grazing flocks, Moses often thought about his people in Egypt. In the freedom of the wide horizons of the pasturelands Moses brooded over the plight of his people who were slaves in Egypt. The more he brooded, the more he became convinced that it was wrong for people to allow others to be slaves.

As long as my people are slaves, Moses thought, I cannot feel free. I am free, and they are slaves. It is my duty to go and free my people, Moses concluded.

When his mind was fully made up, and his plans completed, Moses left his wife and children behind in Midian and returned to Egypt, his birthplace.

Together with his brother Aaron he appeared before the King of Egypt and demanded that his people the Hebrews be freed from slavery.

"Who sent you here to demand the freedom of the Hebrews?" the King asked.

"The Lord God of the Hebrews sent me to you, saying, 'Let my people go that they may serve me in the wilderness!' "

Pharaoh opened his Book of Gods and began to read. He read the names of all the gods of Egypt, and all the gods of Edom, and all the gods of Moab, and all the other gods. He read the Book of Gods from beginning to end. Then he shook his head and said:

"I cannot find the name of your god in my book. I shall not let the Hebrews go from my land!"

When Moses came to Egypt, legend has it, he took the rod he found in Jethro's garden along with him.

When Pharaoh refused to free the Hebrew slaves, Aaron whispered to his brother:

"What can we do now, Moses?"

"Fear not," replied Moses and pointed to the rod in his hand. "You see that the first letter in the first word Detzach is D."

"What does that mean?"

"That stands for *Daam,* which means blood. Our God will bring the plague of blood upon the Egyptians."

Then Moses turned to Pharaoh and said:

"Hear, O Pharaoh! With this rod I'll turn all the water in Egypt into blood before your very eyes!"

"Let me see you do it!" said Pharaoh, for he did not believe a word Moses said.

Moses turned the rod in a certain way, and at once all the brooks and streams and lakes and rivers in Egypt were turned into blood. Wherever there had been water before there was now blood.

Still Pharaoh refused to let the Hebrews go.

Moses looked at the rod, saw the next letter that meant: Frogs. One turn of the rod, in a certain way, and all Egypt became covered with frogs.

Then Moses looked at his rod and turned it in a certain way and brought down upon the Land of Egypt vermin the size of eggs; and swarms of flies; and hail; and locusts; and darkness.

When Pharaoh still refused to let the Hebrews go, Moses raised his rod, in a certain way, and brought down upon the Egyptians the last plague: the death of the firstborn.

At last Pharaoh was frightened. He was a firstborn son himself, and afraid he might die. So he permitted the Hebrews to leave Egypt.

But whatever methods Moses really used, he finally persuaded King Pharaoh to free the Hebrews, and orders were issued to let the Hebrews leave the land. And some 3200 years ago Moses led his people out of bondage.

They were a large army travelling on horseback, in carts, and on foot, following their leader Moses eastwards —Out of Bondage and to the Promised Land. The Promised Land, Moses told his people, was a land flowing milk and honey, promised to the Hebrews by a god called Jehovah.

Before going to the Promised Land in the north, Moses led his people to Mount Sinai in the south, to make a covenant between Jehovah and the freed children of Israel.

In Egypt there were many gods and idols, and people who wished to see their gods could do so by going to the nearest temple. The freed Israelites thought that at the foot of Mount Sinai they would find their god in the form of a bull, a calf, or an owl. And they were very disappointed to see nothing but a mountain.

"Where is this god you have told us about and who promised to bring us safely to the Promised Land?" the people demanded.

"Unlike any other god is Jehovah!" Moses replied. "For they who see the face of Jehovah must die!"

Then Moses went up to the top of the mountain and remained there for forty days. After forty days he came down with what is known as:

The Ten Commandments of Jehovah

These Commandments ordered the Israelites:

To have no other gods than Jehovah;

To worship no idol or image of any kind;

Not to take the name of Jehovah in vain;

To rest every seventh day in the week and call that day Holy;

To honor their fathers and their mothers;

Never to commit murder;

Never to commit adultery;

Not to steal;

Not to swear falsely or give false testimony;

And not to envy other people and covet what they have.

These Commandments did not all teach new ideas. The Egyptians knew and taught some of these ideas, also.

There were, however, two Commandments that had never been heard of before by the Tribes of Israel.

Slaves in Egypt worked every day in the year, and now Moses commanded his people, in the name of Jehovah:

"Six days shalt thou labor and do all thy work, but the Seventh day is the Day of Rest."

But the most important Commandment of all was the very first.

"I am Jehovah thy God which have brought thee out of the land of Egypt out of the house of bondage: Thou shalt have no other gods before me."

In this First Commandment it is not said that Jehovah was the *only* god in the world. What it said was that the Children of Israel should have no other gods but Jehovah.

Just, for instance, as when a man becomes a citizen of the United States, he swears allegiance to this land *only*. There are, of course, many other countries in the world, but this man swears to have nothing to do with any but this country.

And so the First Commandment made the Children of Israel swear allegiance to Jehovah. It was an agreement between Jehovah and the Israelites: They would be Jehovah's Chosen People; and Jehovah would be their Only God.

They were now ready to move on to the Promised Land in the North.

Moses ordered an ark to be made, covered with gold and silver. This he called the Ark of the Covenant. In this Ark, he told his people, now dwelt the Spirit of the god Jehovah.

With the Ark of the Covenant the Israelites turned northward, and for many years wandered through the desert toward the Jordan and the land beyond the Jordan that was Canaan.

6. THE RISE OF THE UNITED HEBREW KINGDOM

Believing that Jehovah their god was fighting their battles with them, the Tribes of Israel showed great courage. With song on their lips and faith in their hearts the Tribes of Israel conquered the Moabites and the Amorites and the Kingdom of Bashan. The story of their victories went before them like a mighty army and conquered their enemies before they were tried by the sword.

Such is the story of the conquest of Canaan by the Israelites who came from barren deserts to the fertile land of Canaan, called Palestine.

But when the Children of Israel settled on the land and became tillers of the soil and growers of the olive and the grape, a change came over them. For the ways and thoughts of wandering desert tribes are different from the ways and thoughts of farmers.

A farmer knows the joy of seeding and the joy of reaping. He knows the sorrow of too much rain, and the sorrow of clear skies when clouds are prayed for. A farmer sings jubilant songs when gathering in the harvest. And he groans mournfully when a pestilence befalls his crops.

This change of the farmer came over the wandering

Israelites. To their songs and prayers were added many agricultural songs and prayers. And to their religious holidays, they added the holidays celebrating the important events in a farmer's life.

There is still another way in which farmers differ from wandering tribes:

A wanderer has no neighbors. But farmers have neighbors whose ways they must learn to understand.

Neighbors may be friends, and again they may be enemies. If they are friends, their friendship has to be kept. And if they are enemies, they must be distrustfully watched.

Because the Children of Israel changed from nomads to farmers, and the problems of their lives changed, their God Jehovah, too, had to change with them.

In the desert Jehovah was a wandering god of a wandering people, fighting their battles and vanquishing their enemies.

But in the land of Canaan his followers looked to him to protect them from unfriendly neighbors in a peaceful way, and to give them rain in season, and wind in season, and sunshine in season.

Jehovah was no longer a wandering god housed in a little wooden ark, but the god of the people of the land:

Jehovah, God of the Land of Palestine.

At first the people of Israel in Palestine were ruled by Judges, who were their military leaders. But after three hundred years of the rule of the Judges, the Twelve Tribes of Israel organized into a Kingdom, and a farmer named Saul was chosen as their first King.

The United Kingdom of Israel did not last long. It had only three kings: Saul, David, and Solomon.

Yet during the rule of these three kings the glory of Israel as a Kingdom reached its height.

It was during the rule of the Third King, Solomon, that a temple was built in the city of Jerusalem, called the Temple of God. In that Temple there was a place called the Holy of Holies. And there, in the Holy of Holies, dwelt Jehovah, God of the land of Palestine and Protector of the United Hebrew Kingdom.

7. THE FALL OF THE UNITED HEBREW KINGDOM

King Saul established the Kingdom.

King David strengthened it and widened its borders.

King Solomon enriched it.

After Solomon died the people of the United Hebrew Kingdom disagreed amongst themselves. The people of the North claimed that David and Solomon and their ministers who lived in the South of Palestine did not treat the northern people as their own. And they decided to establish a kingdom of their own.

And so there came to be two kingdoms in Palestine: the Kingdom of Israel in the North; and the Kingdom of Judah in the South.

The division of the small land into two kingdoms weakened them against enemies. Only about two-hundred years after the death of Solomon the Assyrians conquered the Kingdom of Israel, and its people were taken captive to other lands.

Many books have been written about the conquered people of the Kingdom of Israel, and many legends told about them, because no trace of them has been left anywhere. They are always referred to as the Ten Lost Tribes of Israel.

The Kingdom of Judah in the South was better prepared to fight its enemies and lasted about 160 years longer than the Kingdom in the North.

Then the Babylonians came down upon them, destroyed the cities, burned the Temple in Jerusalem, and carried away thousands of the people of Judah into captivity in Babylon.

The Israelites, a people freed from slavery in Egypt, came marching to their Promised Land with bright hopes and gay songs. After about seven hundred years they were led away from their Promised Land to be slaves once more, their hearts hopeless and their lips silenced by sorrow.

The Kingdom of Israel went under like a ship sunk in mid-ocean, leaving no trace behind it. And with the destruction of the Kingdom of Judah by the Babylonians the history of the Children of Israel might have come to its last chapter.

But as they were led into captivity, something strange happened to the belief of the captives.

As long as they were in their own land they thought of Jehovah as the God of Palestine.

But now that they were being dispersed amongst the nations, and the Holy City was destroyed, and the House of God was turned into ashes, where was Jehovah their Lord?

The Children of Israel believed that their sorrows were due to their sins and that Jehovah was punishing them as they had been warned. But they were still His Chosen People, and He was still their Only God.

Surely Jehovah was with them in their captivity!

Now, if Jehovah was with his people who were left behind in Palestine, and if He was also with his people who were carried off North and South and East and West, then *Jehovah must be everywhere!*

This realization that their god was everywhere came as a great discovery to the Children of Israel, and later helped change their old religion completely.

8. THE GATHERED HARVEST

Babylon rejoiced over its conquest of Palestine and the Kingdom of Judah. But in those days in Northwestern Asia the hawk that dived down on the rabbit had to beware of the talons of the eagle that might swoop down on both of them.

The victorious Babylonians, about fifty years after they destroyed the Kingdom of Judah, fell into the power of the Persians.

The Persians called the people of the Kingdom of Judah, *Jehudis,* from which we get the word *Jews.* And their religion they called *Judaism.*

The Persians were friendly towards the Jews, and their king, Cyrus, permitted them to return to their land and rebuild their kingdom. And because the Persians were so friendly, the Jews studied the Persian religion, and learned many things from them.

The Persians at that time were Zoroastrians, followers of the teachings of the Prophet Zoroaster. From Zoroastrianism the Jews learned that the Persians believed the world to be ruled by Two Forces: The Good and Wise Lord; and the Evil Spirit.

The Jews could not conceive of a Creator divided in Two. They believed that only One God created both light and darkness, joy and sorrow, good and evil.

The Jews had already concluded that Jehovah must be everywhere. Now they concluded that that One God who created the Universe was none other than Jehovah their God.

Jehovah, the god of several tribes, protector of the land of Palestine and the Kingdom of the House of David, became:

Jehovah, Creator of the World, the Only Lord and Ruler of the Universe.

Through their study of Zoroastrianism the Jews not only reached this very important conclusion that there was only One God in the world, but they also learned other very vital teachings that changed their old religion.

One of these was the belief in Life after Death. From Zoroastrianism the Jews, for the first time, learned of Heaven and Hell, and they carried this belief into their religion.

A much more important belief that the Jews borrowed from Zoroastrianism was their changed conviction about the Coming of the Messiah.

When the power of the Jewish Kingdom weakened, and their enemies conquered and oppressed them, the Jews began to hope for the coming of a Redeemer of Palestine, a national hero, a descendant of King David, who would restore the United Hebrew Kingdom as it had been in the days of David and Solomon.

From the Persians the Jews learned that they, too, awaited a *Sayoshant,* a Redeemer. But the Redeemer of the Zoroastrians was not to be just a national hero who would bring glory and power to the Persians. Their *Sayoshant* would redeem all of mankind from the powers of the Evil Spirit.

The Jews, too, began to think of their Messiah, their Redeemer, as more than just a national hero who would restore the Jewish Kingdom to its glory. Though they still believed that the True Messiah would be a descendant of King David and that he would gather all the Jews together again in their Promised Land, they also began to believe that their Messiah would bring happiness and peace to all the world. Not only the people of the world would live peacefully and happily, but even the animals in the woods and the jungles would make peace. The wolf and the lamb, the leopard and the kid, the lion and the calf would all be friendly neighbors.

By the time the Jews returned to Palestine and, with the help of King Cyrus, rebuilt their Holy Temple in Jerusalem, their religion had greatly changed.

A man known as Ezra the Scribe began collecting the histories, legends and laws of the Jews into books. These collected works were called *The Book, The Bible,* and became the Sacred Scriptures of Judaism.

The happiness of the Jews in their restored homeland did not last long.

As the power of the Persians fell before the greater power of their enemies, the Jews began to suffer oppression again. They were a small, weak and defenceless little nation that could not protect themselves from invasion by the strong powers rising in the West.

First they were conquered by the Greeks.

Then came the Romans to rule them with an iron hand.

The greater the oppression, the more hopeful the Jews became that their Messiah would arrive to redeem them from their suffering.

Their struggle against the many enemies of Israel lasted for about two hundred years, and finally Jerusalem was destroyed again, the Second Temple of God was burned, and the Jews scattered over many lands.

The last days of the Jews in their own land were in 70 A.D., nearly 1900 years ago.

During these 1900 years Judaism has changed. But its important beliefs remain the same.

There are many ways in which Judaism differs from all other living religions in the world.

Judaism was the first religion in history to teach that there was only One God.

Judaism, too, teaches that the Good Life can be led only in a community. A man must always think of his fellow men. And whatever one does, he must think of how it would affect other people.

Even when a Jew wants to pray, he must seek a gathering of at least nine other co-religionists in prayer.

Another difference between Judaism and other living religions is that the important teachings of their Faith were not established by one leader. *It is not a personally founded religion.*

Buddhism, as we have seen, is the religion the Buddha founded, though it changed greatly after his death.

Jainism is the religion Mahavira the Jina founded.

The Poet Kabir founded the Kabir Panthis.

Confucius founded the religion called Confucianism.

Taoism is the religion founded by the Old Philosopher, Lao-tze.

But Judaism has no single founder.

There are many people who believe that Moses is the founder of Judaism. But that is not quite true.

The first man to lay the cornerstone of Judaism was Abraham, who said: *Idols must not be worshipped.*

Moses added to this religion the Ten Commandments and the belief that the Jews were Jehovah's Chosen People.

In Palestine the ideas of Judaism grew one by one. From Zoroastrianism, many centuries later, the Jews borrowed many teachings and incorporated them, in a changed form, into their own religion.

And so Judaism grew and developed with the growth and development of the Jewish People.

That is why the story of the Jewish Religion is so much the story of the Jewish People.

Judaism was not so much a Faith, as a Law of Living; it was not only the religion of the Jews, but also their way of life.

That is one of the reasons why, though Judaism was the oldest of the great monotheistic religions, it did not become a Universal Religion. For Judaism was concerned with the experiences of its own people; and the experiences of the Jews throughout the centuries became part of the Judaic heritage. Zion became to them physically and symbolically their Holy Mountain.

9.   THE PROPHETS OF ISRAEL

Often, when the Jews were in their homeland, their rulers became corrupt and their leaders turned away from the Holy Law and the teachings of their religion. Many of the people began to imitate the ways of their conquerors, and some even turned to idolatry.

At such times, certain men arose who would call upon the people to return to their Law, and in the name of Jehovah they would foretell what would happen to Israel if they failed to follow the ways of righteousness as taught by their religion. These men were called Prophets. And whenever the Jews were in trouble, the Prophets arose to teach the people the Ways of the Lord.

There were many prophets in Israel. From the time Abraham offended his people by saying that idols must not be worshipped and had to flee from Chaldea to

Canaan, the troubles of the Jews began. And as time went on their troubles increased. No wonder, then, that Israel had so many Prophets!

The Prophets would explain to the people the reasons for their troubles, and urge them to turn from their evil ways to the way of God and good. The Prophets were wise men, and they knew that from good must come good.

The corrupt kings disliked the Prophets.

The Priests hated them.

And the people showed little love for these inspired men.

But the Prophets did not stop warning the people to turn from their evil ways. Was what they said true and was it just? they asked. If it was true and just, then not even the threat of death could silence them. Most of the Prophets were poor. They came from the hills of Judaea to the market-places and to the Temple. And wherever they could gather an audience they spoke their minds.

Up to the time when the Jews were taken captives to Babylon, the Prophets were Israel's Divine Statesmen.

The King and his court looked after the Laws of the Land.

The Priests looked after the Laws of the Temple.

The Prophets taught the people the Laws of Truth and Justice.

Not only did the Prophets teach the Jews to follow the good and avoid the evil, but each and every Jew, they said, ought to be a crusader against evil. The Jews had a mission in life, and that was to fight evil and spread the good.

"Lovers of Jehovah," the Prophets commanded, "lovers of Jehovah, hate evil!"

After the return from Babylon the Prophets also began to tell about the Coming of the Messiah—not just an emancipator of Palestine, but an Emancipator of Mankind.

The sermons and teachings of the many Prophets were gathered by scribes, and now they form a great part of the Sacred Scriptures of the Jews.

10. THE FALSE LIGHTS OF THE WANDERERS

In the last war of the Jews on their own soil nearly a million and a half of their people were slain. Their conqueror, Titus Caesar, tore down the walls of Jerusalem and set the Second Temple of God on fire until the very hill on which it was built seemed to have burst into flames.

That marked the close of the great Jewish War, and the beginning of the Jewish Exile. Since then the Jews have spread all over the world.

Whenever the troubles of the Jews seemed too hard to bear, their hope of the coming of the Messiah flickered up. Many times through the centuries of Exile, rumor spread among the Jews that the Messiah had come. These Messiahs, or False Messiahs as they were later called, arose in Persia, in Palestine, in France, in Spain, and in other countries where the Jews dwelt.

The best known of these False Messiahs was one named Shabbatai Zevi.

Zevi was born in Smyrna in 1626, eight years after the Thirty Years' War had begun in Europe. The people all over Europe suffered on account of this long war, and the Jews suffered amongst them.

As year after year of the war passed, and the suffering of the people grew greater and greater, they began to believe that the end of the world had come, and that the war was ushering in the arrival of the Redeemer of Mankind.

In England and in Holland and in France and in Germany many books were written about the Coming of the Redeemer of Mankind.

And the year of His arrival was calculated to be 1666.

The Jews, who believed that the Redeemer would be of the House of David, now hoped that the coming of the Messiah would bring an end to their life in exile, and that they would be led back to their homeland in Palestine.

Many of the stories of the expected Messiah must have been told to Zevi when he was a child. As he grew older he began to study the Book of Daniel in which the coming of the Messiah was foretold. Then he began fasting day after day. And it seems that even as a young boy he began to dream of becoming the expected Redeemer.

And the year 1666 came nearer and nearer.

At the age of twenty-two, when the Thirty Years' War had just ended, Zevi appeared before a group of his friends and announced that he was the True Messiah, Chosen of God to restore Israel to Jerusalem. But no one took him seriously.

Realizing that his people at home would not listen to him, Zevi travelled away to Salonica and proclaimed himself Messiah there. But in Salonica, too, the people would not take him seriously. Zevi left them and went on to Jerusalem. When he found no followers there either, he travelled to Cairo, Egypt. By the time he reached Cairo he was already thirty-four years old.

And the year 1666 drew nearer and nearer.

Zevi remained in Cairo for three years. He gained a few followers who admired his knowledge of mystic books. With some of his admirers Zevi returned to Jerusalem, the Holy City, where he promised to perform great miracles on the Day of Redemption.

In Jerusalem Zevi spent the days in fasting, and the nights in prayer. The people about him slowly began to believe that he was really the Messiah, and gradually Zevi's name became known all over the East, and his fame travelled far and wide.

The year 1665, the last year before the Judgment Day, had begun!

Zevi returned that year to Smyrna, his birthplace, and there a great crowd received him with joy and proclaimed him the Blessed Lord and King, Messiah of the God of Jacob.

The story of his arrival in Smyrna reached Italy, and France, and Germany, and Holland, and Poland, and England.

People put on their best clothes and gathered at the synagogues and meeting places to dance and sing. And many of the rich amongst them gave away their wealth, believing that when the Messiah would reveal himself they would need nothing but their souls.

Marvelous stories began to circulate amongst the people. One told of a strange and wonderful ship that suddenly appeared in northern Scotland. This ship had sails and ropes of silk, and was manned by sailors who spoke Hebrew. And it flew a flag bearing these words:

"The Twelve Tribes of Israel."

The joy of the Jews everywhere was beyond bounds. And even many religious Christians believed that Zevi was the Expected Redeemer of Mankind.

And the year 1666 drew near.

As a sign that he was the true Messiah, Zevi sent word to his people that the Tenth of Tebet, which the Jews observe as a day of sorrow and fasting, should be changed into a Holiday. The message read:

"The first-begotten Son of God, Shabbatai Zevi, Messiah and Redeemer of the People of Israel, to all sons of Israel, Peace!

"Since you have been deemed worthy to behold the great day and the fulfilment of God's word to the Prophets, your lament and sorrow must be changed to joy, and your fasting into merriment; for ye shall weep no more. Rejoice with song and melody, and change the day formerly spent in sadness and sorrow into a day of Jubilee, because I have appeared."

This message strengthened the faith of the people everywhere. Surely the Messiah had come, if he could change the days of sorrow and fasting into Holidays and Festivities.

And the year 1666 began to dawn!

The Jews the world over almost held their breath, waiting for Jehovah to restore his people to their homeland by a great miracle.

In that much awaited year, Zevi, instead of going south to Jerusalem from Smyrna, went north to Constantinople.

As soon as he arrived there he was arrested by the command of the Sultan and placed in prison. On September 16, 1666, Zevi was brought before the Sultan and told that he must choose between accepting the religion of the Turks, or being executed for treason.

Shabbatai Zevi accepted the religion of the Turk.

The joy of the Jewish people expecting the Messiah turned into great grief and sorrow.

11. THE UNDYING HOPE

But the hope of the Jews to return to Palestine did not die.

Though most of them gave up the hope of being led back to Jerusalem through a miracle, they planned their redemption in the form of a movement called *Zionism*.

The hope of returning to what the Jews always called the "Land of Israel" never really died down. Though they were so often disappointed by the false Messiahs, they continued to hope and to dream.

Then, toward the end of the 19th Century, Jews the world over were startled by the appearance of a book, called "The Jewish State," and written by a Viennese writer Dr. Theodor Herzl. On the title page of his book Dr. Herzl wrote:

"If you will it, it need not remain a dream."

Only one year after his book appeared, Dr. Herzl summoned the first World Congress of Zionism. At this historic meeting in Switzerland, where Jewish delegates from every corner of the earth assembled, Dr. Herzl prophesied that within fifty years Israel will be restored and the Jews will take their place as a nation among the nations.

As he prophesied, so it happened.

Fifty years after the first Zionist Congress the new Jewish State, called *Israel,* was established.

On May 14, 1948, David Ben-Gurion, leader in Israel, arose in the Tel-Aviv Art Museum to read in Hebrew the Jewish Declaration of Independence. When he finished, an orchestra played the Jewish National Anthem, the *Hatikvoh* (The Hope).

The *Hatikvoh* had been fulfilled.

Said Ben-Gurion: "Our State has been established."

Judaism in the U.S.A.

The four thousand Jewish congregations in the United States are unevenly divided among the Orthodox, Conservative and Reform (or Liberal) denominations.

All the movements and denominations of Judaism in America had their origin in other lands, excepting one: *Reconstructionism.* This is an American movement, organized by Dr. Mordecai M. Kaplan in the 1930s, which seeks to reconstruct Jewish life and adapt it to 20th century America.

Dr. Kaplan views Judaism as a dynamic religious civilization, which, in America, must be lived simultaneously with the primary civilization of our land; and he has established basic principles as to how this can be accomplished.

Part Three: CHRISTIANITY

STAR OF THE PURPLE EAST

> *"By this shall all men know
> that you are my disciples—if
> you have love for one another."*
>
> From *The Last Commandment
> of Jesus*

FOUNDED: 30 A.D.

FOUNDER: Jesus of Nazareth, called *The Christ* (6 B.C.?-A.D. 29-30?)

PLACE: Palestine (now Israel)

SACRED SCRIPTURES: The *Old* and the *New Testaments;* and to these, large segments of Christianity add the *Apocrypha. The Old Testament,* excepting for a difference in the order of the material, is the same as the Hebrew Scriptures. *The New Testament* consists of the Story of Jesus as told in the four *Gospels;* the formation of the Church as told in the *Acts* and the *Epistles;* and *Revelation,* which is an apocalyptic work. The *Apocrypha* consist of fourteen miscellaneous works which form a bridge between the *Old* and the *New Testaments*.

NUMBER OF ADHERENTS: 800,000,000

DISTRIBUTION: Christians are to be found the world over. They predominate in North and South America and in Europe.

CHRISTIANS IN THE UNITED STATES: There are nearly one hundred million Christians affiliated in churches, of nearly 250 denominations.

SECTS: Christianity is divided into: The Greek Orthodox; The Roman Catholic; and the Protestant. There are some 250 Protestant denominations.

CHRISTIANITY:

STAR OF THE PURPLE EAST

1. THE HOPE OF THE JEWS

From the time Moses led his people out of bondage, the Jews believed that in time of need their God Jehovah would send them a Deliverer who would triumph over their enemies and who would bring them the blessings of eternal Justice and Peace.

This hoped-for Deliverer was called the Messiah: The Anointed One.

Never in the history of the Jews was their hope of the coming of the Messiah so great as in the days of Augustus Caesar, about a hundred years before Palestine was completely conquered by the Romans. The suffering of the Jews at that time was very great, and the people hoped that their troubles were the sign of the coming of the Deliverer.

A little book of less than thirty pages, called the Book of Daniel, was being read and discussed by everyone.

In this curious little book Daniel told of many strange dreams he had dreamt.

In one dream he saw four great beasts come up from the sea. One looked like a lion with eagle's wings. One was like a very hungry bear. Another was like a leopard with four heads and four wings. But the most terrible of all was the fourth beast. It had iron teeth and nails of brass, and ten horns upon its head. There were eyes in those horns as well as mouths that could speak. And those mouths in the horns of the beast did say some very terrible things.

In another dream Daniel saw a ram come up from a river. The ram had two horns, two high horns, two powerful horns which he swung to the west and to the north and to the south, and no beast dared oppose him. Until a he-goat appeared in the west, a powerful he-goat with only one horn between his eyes. And he attacked the ram and trampled him under his feet.

These, and many other dreams Daniel had, which he

could not understand. But an angel came to him and explained to him the meaning of his dreams.

The time is coming, the angel said, when the Son of Man, from the House of David, will come to establish the Kingdom of Heaven on earth and bring happiness and peace to the world.

How soon that would be the angel did not say.

But once Daniel overheard an angel predict that the time of the coming of the Messiah would be after "a time, and times, and half a time."

Just when "a time, and times, and half a time" would be Daniel did not know.

Yet this was exactly what the people who later read his little book of strange dreams tried to find out. And many calculations were made.

In the little Book of Daniel it was also said that before the Messiah arrives 'there shall be a time of trouble, such as never was since there was a nation.'

This time of trouble, the Jews under the Roman Rule thought, had surely come. Many of them expected the Chosen One to arrive any day of their lives. So certain were they that the coming of the Messiah was to be very soon, that some of them gave away all their earthly possessions, left their wives and their homes and their children and their work, and went about fasting and praying in order to prepare themselves for the Great Day.

In the synagogues, in the market-places, and in the homes all over the land the coming of the Messiah was discussed. The learned as well as the lowly, the old as well as the young, everywhere, discussed the Coming of the Messiah.

"The Messiah! The Messiah! His day is near! Blessed be the name of the Lord!"

So people whispered to each other. Some called him the Anointed One. Some called him Son of Man. Some called him Son of David. And some spoke of him in whispers as the Son of God.

What will the Messiah look like when he comes?

How will the people be able to recognize him?

Will he be born of woman, or will he come down directly from Heaven on the Fiery Chariot that took up Elijah the Prophet?

These questions the people asked.

And the learned amongst them described the Messiah, and said:

"The Son of David will appear on a mountain top with a crown of glory upon his head, led under a canopy by Elijah the Prophet and a host of angels."

"But exactly where will the Messiah appear?" some asked.

"He will appear in the North," some answered.

"He will appear in the South," others answered.

And still others said:

"The Son of David will appear with the clouds of Heaven and descend upon the roof of the Holy Temple in Jerusalem."

But no matter how they disagreed as to *where* the Messiah would appear, and *how* he would appear, they all agreed that he was soon to come. And the talk of his coming was forever on their lips.

2. ONE BAD KING AND THREE WISE MEN

In those days the true ruler of Judea was Augustus Caesar, the Roman Emperor. But Judea also had a king of its own. He was not a Jew. He was not a Roman. He was not a Greek. He was a mixture of several races, including the Philistinian. If he had not been a king, he would have gone unnoted. But being a king, he was called King Herod the Great.

King Herod, we are told, was a very bad king. That we can readily believe. Since the earth was created there have been many, many kings upon it. If the names and titles of all the kings that ever lived were written down in one straight line, their names would reach the moon or even farther than that. Yet it would be hard to find enough names of *good* kings to fill a page—even a small page. And so we can readily believe that King Herod the Great was a bad king.

Though his life in the palace was not a very happy one, yet King Herod wished to remain ruler of Judea for ever and ever. And nothing made him angrier than the talk of the people about the coming of the Messiah, Son of David, who would become King of the Jews.

One day, and King Herod was then almost seventy years old, a royal spy came to the palace and said:

"Your Majesty! Three Wise Men from Persia have arrived in Jerusalem, laden with treasures. They go about the city asking, 'Where is the child that has been born to become the King of the Jews? We have come to worship him!' "

"Bring these Wise Men to me at once!" the King commanded.

And when the Wise Men, called Magi, were brought before the king, he asked them:

"What sign have you that the expected Son of David, King of the Jews, has been born?"

And the Magi answered and said:

"We saw a star arise in the east and it moved before us until we came here. That was our sign."

The evil king thought for a while in his evil mind, then said:

"Go and find the child that has been born to be King of the Jews. And when you have found him, bring me word where he is that I, too, may go and worship him."

The Three Wise Men left the king, so the story tells, and followed the purple star they had seen rise in the east. The star moved before them and the Magi followed it. They followed it out of Jerusalem, and far away to Bethlehem. There the star stopped over a dwelling where at that time were housed a carpenter named Joseph, his wife Mary, and her newly-born son, Jesus.

The Three Wise Men entered the house, kneeled before the infant in his mother's lap, and spread at the mother's feet the treasures of gold, frankincense and myrrh they had brought with them. Then the Magi left Bethlehem.

But they did not return to Jerusalem. These Magi were wise men and they understood that King Herod wanted to find out where the child was, not to worship him, but to harm him. And so they left for their homes in Persia, without returning to the Palace of King Herod the Great.

That night Joseph the Carpenter dreamt that King Herod had sent messengers to Bethlehem to kill the infant Jesus. Joseph was so frightened by that dream, that the very next day he took his wife and child and fled to Egypt.

Meanwhile King Herod waited for the Three Wise Men to return and tell him where they had found the child born to be King of the Jews. He waited and waited, and the longer he waited the angrier he became. At last, when he realized that those Magi would never return, he began to think of ways of killing that child. Since he did not know which child in Bethlehem it was, King Herod ordered all the boys in that city two years old and under to be killed.

There is one nice thing about all bad kings; sooner or later they die. And Herod the Great died soon after Joseph and his family had fled to Egypt.

When the news of the king's death reached Egypt, so the story tells, Joseph returned with his family to the land of his birth and settled in the town of Nazareth, in the Province of Galilee.

3. IN THE TOWN OF NAZARETH

Nazareth in Lower Galilee was a small out-of-the-way town, far from the Highways of the Nations, hidden in a valley and surrounded by rolling hills. The houses in the town were all built of white stone brought from the quarries nearby. At a distance, the whiteness of the stone buildings, clinging to the sloping hill, seemed dazzling in the sun, and people called Nazareth "The White City."

Nazareth was only about fifty-five miles from Jerusalem. But in those days, when the donkey was employed as a fast express, the din of the big city did not reach the rustic little town in the hills of Galilee.

All those who could afford it, in those days in Palestine, sent their children to Jerusalem to receive their education from the great Rabbis. Joseph the Carpenter could not afford it. But as he worked in his carpenter-shop he taught Jesus all the Holy Commandments; and Mary taught him the morning and evening prayers. And in the synogogue, on Sabbaths and during the many holidays, Jesus heard readings from the Bible and learned much about the Holy Law and the customs that good Jews must follow.

According to some writers on the childhood of Jesus, there was nothing unusual to be noted about the boy when he was very young. Others, however, have filled many long volumes (called Apocryphal Gospels) which describe in great detail many miraculous deeds performed by Jesus in his early childhood. Many of the stories told in the apocryphal books are concerned with the education of Jesus.

According to one story, the boy Jesus had an inquisitive mind and a great love for learning. He was taken to one rabbi who was to teach him the alphabet; and he soon astonished his teacher by reciting all the letters in the alphabet, the symbolical meaning of their shapes, and mystical reason for each letter being placed in its appointed place in the alphabet.

Jesus was a dreamy child who loved to linger in the synagogue and listen to the older men discuss the Bible, and exchange stories about Rabbi Hillel the Old, who had lived some fifty years before.

It is told that once a heathen came to Rabbi Hillel the Old, and asked: "Can you teach me all of the Holy Law whilst I stand on one foot?" To which Rabbi Hillel replied: "What is hateful to you, do not do unto others—that is the whole of the Holy Law!"

This, and many other stories like it Jesus heard in the synagogues of Nazareth. More pleasant to him than the games in the fields were these simple stories. But what he liked most were the whispered talks about the coming of the Messiah who would fill the hearts of all those laden with sorrow with an everlasting joy.

When Jesus reached his twelfth birthday a great change took place in his life. For at that age he became confirmed, and had to be instructed in the Law. One of the most important obligations of the confirmed was the yearly pilgrimage to Jerusalem to observe the Passover Feast. And in the year of his confirmation Jesus left Nazareth for the first time in his life to go up to Jerusalem, capital of Palestine.

Poor and rich, old and young from all over Palestine went up to Jerusalem for the Passover. They who had camels and donkeys rode; the rest went on foot.

Joseph the carpenter was too poor to own even a donkey. So Jesus had to walk with his parents the entire distance from Nazareth in Galilee, through Samaria, down to Jerusalem, over fifty-five miles away.

On the way they met many other pilgrims from other parts of the land. The nearer they came to Jerusalem the greater swelled the number of pilgrims. Until, when they came within sight of the city, they formed a mighty army of men, women and children coming to serve Jehovah in his Temple.

Jesus had heard much about Jerusalem, and he had often tried to imagine the splendor of the City of God. Arriving now in the midst of a vast army of pilgrims, he was fascinated when against the skyline appeared the first outline of the far-famed Jerusalem, thrice conquered Jerusalem, proud City of God.

But as soon as they entered the city, Jesus realized that Jerusalem was unlike the city of his dreams. Everywhere about him he heard foreign languages spoken; he saw a mixture of foreign people dressed in foreign clothes; and frowning centurions and Roman soldiers everywhere amongst the crowds.

Even greater was his disappointment when they reached the Temple. The House of God, of which he had so often thought with reverence and awe, he found surrounded by herds of bleating sheep and lowing oxen offered for sale to the arriving worshippers as the necessary sacrifices. And everywhere amongst the noisy crowds of cattle-dealers and haggling pilgrims, money-changers shouted their readiness to exchange the moneys used in the various parts of the land for the silver currency of Jerusalem.

But the worst disappointment of all came to Jesus when he entered that part of the Temple where the Great Rabbis assembled to discuss the Holy Law.

At home, in the little synagogue of Nazareth, the Law was simple and easy to understand. But here in the Temple Jesus listened to long and difficult interpretations. The words were familiar to him, yet their meaning was hard to grasp.

After the celebration of the Passover was over, Jesus returned with his parents to the simple and quiet life of Nazareth. But his dreams of the glory of the City of God had crumbled. The memory of the Holy Temple surrounded by a noisome market-place saddened him. It was not always so, he told himself, and it should not always be that way.

He became interested in the Book of Daniel, and all other books that foretold the Coming of the Messiah. More than ever he kept to himself, thinking and dreaming about the expected Redeemer of Mankind.

4. THE MEETING OF JESUS AND JOHN

From the time Jesus first went up to Jerusalem in his twelfth year until he was nearly thirty years old we know little of his life. All we know is that Joseph died, and that Mary, his mother, moved with her family from Nazareth to Cana, her birthplace.

There Jesus followed the trade he had learned, carpentry, and helped support his family.

All week long Jesus worked with hammer and plane in his little shop in the village of Cana. And on Sabbaths he went to the synagogue for prayer and discussion of the Holy Law.

Often he arose before the worshippers to explain the Law. Such was the custom in those days in Palestine. They who felt so moved arose before the congregation to interpret and explain whatever part of the Law they had given thought to. But the interpretations of Jesus were unlike the interpretations of others. His words were simple and appealed to the hearts of his listeners. Many in the synagogue became his admirers and called him *Rabeinu,* meaning: Our Teacher. And many of them began to discuss the teachings of the young carpenter of Cana.

About this time stories were being told about a young man named John, the son of one Zacharias and his wife Elizabeth, who came from Judea to the banks of the Jordan to announce the *Gospel,* which means: The Good Tidings.

The Good Tidings in Palestine, then, was the prophecy that the Messiah was soon to appear.

A large number of followers had gathered about John near Bethabara on the Jordan, it was reported, and there John immersed them in the water of the river to sanctify them before preaching to them about the Coming of the Messiah.

For centuries people all over Asia believed that there is a mystic power in flowing water. In India, as we have seen, people go to the Ganges to bathe in it, believing that the water of this sacred river can wash their sins away.

Some of the Jews in the days of Jesus also believed that immersion in flowing water cleansed people of their sins. John, too, believed in that. And he baptized people in the Jordan before he preached to them. That was why he was called John the Baptist.

Though John preached in Judea in the South, his fame travelled down to Galilee in the North, and reached Cana.

Jesus left his shop and went south to meet the Baptist who, Mary said, was his third cousin.

On the banks of the Jordan, not far from Jericho, Jesus met a large number of men surrounding one, wearing a coat of camel's hair tied with a cord about his loins, who addressed them with fiery words. Though he was only a young man of about thirty years, his beard was long and his hair neglected. From his appearance and his words Jesus knew that that must be the Baptist of whom he had heard.

Jesus neared and heard John say:

"There cometh one mightier than I after me, the latchet of whose shoes I am not worthy to stoop down to unloose!"

At the end of the sermon Jesus went up to John and asked to be baptized. But the discerning eye of the prophet saw at once that Jesus was no ordinary follower. John hesitated.

"I have need to be baptized by you, and you come to me?"

But Jesus insisted, and John baptized him.

The meeting of Jesus with John, in the thirtieth year of his life, marked the beginning of his prophetic career—a career which was to last only three years, three eventful years rapidly moving to the Sorrowful End.

5. THE SERMON ON THE MOUNT

For years Jesus had read and heard about the Coming of the Messiah. In all the books and all the whispered stories the Redeemer seemed only a dream of the sorrowful. But from the lips of John came the clear announcement that the Coming of the Redeemer was nigh. There was no doubt in John's heart, no question in John's utterances. The Coming of the Messiah, soon, quite soon, was as certain as the coming of the dawn when the night has passed.

Jesus left John and went away into the desert of Judea to think about the Messiah John had prophesied. For forty days he remained in the vast loneliness of the desert in prayer and meditation.

From the desert Jesus returned home, his thoughts on a Brotherhood of Man and a world all Justice and Peace. But he did not remain long in Galilee. For the Passover was approaching, the time for the annual pilgrimage to Jerusalem.

Jesus went down to the Holy City for the yearly Feast. Still wrapped up in thoughts of the Kingdom of Heaven, he arrived in the court of the Temple. And there before him once more was the sight of oxen and bound sheep, eager merchants and dealers in doves, niggardly money-changers squatting before their little tables laden with coins, and the pilgrims come to glorify Jehovah moving about and haggling with the dealers.

Jesus looked up at the Temple in which rested the Holy of Holies, then turned his eyes again to the market-place. A great resentment rose within him for this irreverence toward the House of God.

He picked up a whip that one of the cattle-dealers had dropped and drove the cattle out of the court, overturned the tables of the money-changers, spreading the rolling coins over the pebbled yard. And above the noise of the startled merchants, the voice of Jesus rose:

"Take these things hence! Make not God's House a market-place!"

Nothing Jesus could have done would have brought him more to the wrathful attention of the Priests and the religious leaders of Jerusalem. For they had tolerated the merchants in the inner court of the Temple. By driving out the merchants and money-changers Jesus had defied the authority of the Priests.

Through this act Jesus aroused many enemies. But they were few as compared with the friends and followers who flocked to the man who had dared defy the authorities in Jerusalem, and admonish those who had desecrated the Holy Temple.

At the end of the Passover, Jesus returned to Galilee and preached in Nazareth and Cana about the religion that ought to spring from the heart.

The people who had known Jesus from his childhood tried to make light of his teachings.

"Is not this Joseph the carpenter's son?" they said to each other.

"Yes, this is the son of Mary," people replied. "You know his brothers and sisters, don't you?"

"What makes him so wise then?" they mocked.

Jesus, who heard them, said:

"A prophet is not without honor, save in his own country and in his own house."

He left for Capernaum, a little village on the shores of Lake Galilee, and there he lived with two brothers named Peter and Andrew, humble fishermen, who believed that Jesus was the expected Messiah. Very often Jesus went out to the lake shore where the fishermen gathered to mend their nets, and he preached to them there.

Slowly the fame of Jesus grew in Capernaum. And slowly it was carried beyond Capernaum to all the neighboring villages and towns. Marvelous tales began to be told about the young Carpenter of Nazareth. These tales travelled south to the end of the Kingdom. And people from near and far came to the little fishermen's village to see and hear the man about whom so many wondrous tales were told.

Once a great multitude had gathered on one of the hills near Capernaum to hear Jesus preach. He rose before them and preached to them the sermon that has since been known as the *Sermon on the Mount*. In that Sermon he gave them the most important of his teachings, and showed them in which way his teachings differed from the teachings of the Priests and the Rabbis who had come before him.

In that memorable sermon Jesus said:

"Blessed are the poor in spirit: for theirs is the Kingdom of Heaven.

"Blessed are the meek: for they shall inherit the earth.

"Blessed are they which do hunger and thirst after righteousness, for they shall be filled.

"Blessed are the merciful: for they shall obtain mercy.

"Blessed are the pure in heart: for they shall see God.

"Blessed are the peacemakers: for they shall be called the children of God.

"Think not that I am come to destroy the law, or the prophets: I am not come to destroy but to fulfill.

"Ye have heard that it was said by them of old time: 'Thou shalt not kill; and whosoever shall kill shall be in danger of the judgment'; But I say unto you, that whosoever is angry with his brother without a cause shall be in danger of the judgment.

"Ye have heard that it hath been said, 'An eye for an eye, and a tooth for a tooth': But I say unto you, That ye resist not evil; but whosoever shall smite thee on thy right cheek, turn to him the other also.

"Ye have heard that it hath been said, 'Thou shalt love thy neighbor, and hate thine enemy.' But I say unto you, Love your enemies, bless them that curse you, do good to them that hate you, and pray for them which despitefully use you, and persecute you, that you may be the children of your Father which is in heaven: for he maketh his sun to rise on the evil and on the good, and sendeth rain on the just and on the unjust.

"For if ye forgive men their trespasses, your heavenly Father will also forgive you. But if ye forgive not men their trespasses, neither will your Father forgive your trespasses.

"Judge not, that ye be not judged. For with what judgment ye judge, ye shall be judged: and with what measure ye mete, it shall be measured to you again.

"Ask, and it shall be given you; seek and ye shall find; knock, and it shall be opened unto you. For everyone that asketh receiveth; and he that seeketh findeth; and to him that knocketh it shall be opened.

"Therefore all things whatsoever ye would that men should do to you, do ye even so to them; for this is the law and the prophets.

"Even so every good tree bringeth forth good fruit; but a corrupt tree bringeth forth evil fruit. A good tree cannot bring forth evil fruit, neither can a corrupt tree bring forth good fruit.

"Therefore whosoever heareth these sayings of mine, and doeth them, I will liken him unto a wise man, which built his house upon a rock: And the rain descended, and the floods came, and the winds blew, and beat upon that house; and it fell not, for it was founded upon a rock."

In this Sermon on the Mount, and in most of his sermons and parables after that, Jesus emphasized the difference between his teachings and the teachings of Judaism:

Judaism taught LAW;
Jesus taught LOVE.

6. NONE OTHER GREATER THAN THESE

From amongst his followers and disciples, Jesus chose twelve, whom he called his Apostles, and these he sent out to announce the coming of the Messiah.

The apostles went through Galilee preaching to the people of the coming of the Redeemer of Mankind as foretold by the Prophets. And in whispers they said that Jesus of Nazareth was He Who Cometh.

Great multitudes of believers, as well as crowds who were curious, came to Capernaum seeking Jesus and asking to be healed by him. For it had been told everywhere that Jesus was a great healer.

Wherever Jesus went great multitudes followed him, and often he did not even have time to eat.

At this time John the Baptist, who had made strong utterances against the corruption of Herod Antipas, son of King Herod the Great, was put to death. The sad news of John's death reached Jesus in Capernaum.

The first meeting of Jesus with John was the starting point of the career of Jesus. The news of John's death was the turning point in the career of Jesus.

In his life as in his death, John the Baptist influenced his third cousin in Galilee.

John had paid with his life for preaching in Judea. But in his death John had taught that the best fighting-ground is in the enemy's camp. And Jesus decided to go up to Judea, even into Jerusalem, and spread his teachings there.

Jesus knew the danger. Yet he went up to Jerusalem, and to Bethany near Jerusalem, to spread his teachings.

As soon as his presence in Jerusalem became known to the Priests, they began to plot against Jesus.

The greatest enemies of Jesus were the religious leaders of that day in Jerusalem who were called Pharisees. These Pharisees wanted their people to go back to the old religion as taught before the Jewish Exile to Babylon.

They did not believe in Heaven and Hell; they did not believe in life after death; and they opposed any teachings that were contrary to the Mosaic Law or the teachings of the early Prophets.

Jesus' utterances against the Mosaic Law, as in the Sermon on the Mount and afterwards, angered the Pharisees.

But in those days in Jerusalem no man could be forbidden from preaching whatever he pleased, unless he preached against the Roman Government that ruled Palestine, or unless he was guilty of mocking God.

If they could find Jesus guilty of either treason or blasphemy, the Pharisees thought, then it would be easy to stop him from spreading his teachings.

They came to him and asked him many questions in the hope that Jesus would commit himself against the rulers of the land. But when they failed in that, they tried to get him to commit himself as a blasphemer.

One Pharisee asked:

"Which is the first Commandment of all?"

To which Jesus replied:

"The first of all Commandments is, Hear, O Israel, the Lord our God is One God! And the second is: Thou shalt love thy neighbor as thyself. There is none other commandment greater than these!"

Long discussions followed between Jesus and the Teachers of the Law and the Pharisees. The Pharisees argued that the Holy Law must be followed to the letter, and Jesus argued that the religion that is not of the heart is worthless.

Jesus then denounced the Scribes and Pharisees openly, and warned the people against them. And the gap between Jesus and the leaders of the established Jewish religion widened.

7.   THE LAST COMMANDMENT OF JESUS

Three years after Jesus first appeared and drove the merchants and money-changers out of the court of the Temple, he appeared again in Jerusalem for the Passover Feast.

Three years before he had come alone.

This time he arrived in the midst of a multitude who sang as they went down the streets:

"Hosanna! Blessed is he that cometh in the name of the Lord!"

The people of Jerusalem, who knew little of Jesus the Galilean, stopped and asked:

"Who is this man of whom you sing?"

"Jesus the Prophet of Nazareth!" the followers of Jesus answered, and marched on toward the Temple, repeating their song:

"Hosanna! Blessed is he that cometh in the name of the Lord!"

On entering the Temple court, the sight of the cattle-dealers and money-changers again revolted Jesus. And again he drove them from the court.

The Pharisees and Chief Priests became seriously disturbed by the daring of Jesus. When he had come alone they had not feared him. But now that he had a large following, the Priests and Pharisees began to fear his power and influence, and they gathered in secrecy to decide how they could stop Jesus from preaching and his following from growing.

Jesus left the Temple that morning and returned to

Bethany, about two miles east of Jerusalem, where he was staying with friends. His actions that morning and his utterances in the Temple, he knew, had incited the Priests and Pharisees. Jesus recalled the fate of John the Baptist. Several times during the day he told his disciples that he felt his end was near.

His followers could not understand Jesus' forebodings. Secretly they believed that during the coming Passover Jesus would reveal himself as the Messiah. This secret hope made all his followers jubilant.

Jesus alone awaited the holiday with a heavy heart.

From the Mount of Olives near Jerusalem he watched the great crowds of pilgrims arriving in the city. Everywhere preparations were being made for the Passover. A holiday spirit prevailed all over Jerusalem and wherever the Jews congregated. The hearts of the people were joyful in anticipation of the Feast.

Only the heart of Jesus was heavy with forebodings.

The night before the Passover, Jesus and his twelve apostles gathered in the house of one of his followers to have supper together.

After Jesus had seated himself at the head of the table set for the meal, he noticed the rivalry amongst his disciples for the seats of honor nearest their Master.

Jesus immediately left his seat, took a basin of water, and washed the feet of his disciples. The disciples were all astonished to see their Master do that, and some protested. But Jesus said:

"You have striven amongst yourselves for the seat of honor. Now I have given you an example that you should do as I have done. Remember, the servant is not greater than his lord; neither is he that is sent greater than he that sent him."

The disciples understood the rebuke, and they settled to the meal in silence.

There was meat upon the table and wine. But few of them could eat now. There was no joy in their feasting.

As they sat there in silence, Jesus suddenly said:

"Verily I say unto you that one of you shall betray me."

His words frightened the disciples. They looked at each other sorrowfully, and whispered:

"Is it I, Master, is it I?"

"It is one of the twelve that eateth with me," said Jesus.

Then he added: "It were better for my betrayer were he never born."

They all ate in silence. And when the sorrowful meal was over Jesus arose and turned to his disciples. He looked at them with eyes full of tenderness and love, and said:

"Children, I shall be with you only a little while longer. Ye shall seek me, but whither I go you cannot come. So now I say to you:

"A new commandment I give unto you, that you love one another. As I have loved you, so you shall love one another. By this shall all know that you are my disciples —if you have love for one another."

8.   AT THE END OF THE SORROWFUL WAY

That night Jesus went out of the city into a garden called Gethsemane, where he often went for prayer and meditation. On this night all his disciples were with him, excepting Judas the son of Simon who had left them earlier in the evening.

It was late at night when Jesus and his disciples reached the neglected garden, and they were all tired. One by one the disciples fell asleep.

After midnight the silence and darkness of the night in the garden was broken by the arrival of Judas leading a band of officers and soldiers bearing lanterns and torches and weapons.

Jesus came forward to meet the officers.

"Whom do you seek?" he asked them.

"We seek one named Jesus of Nazareth," they answered.

"I am he."

The officers laid hands on Jesus and bound him. The noise in the garden woke the sleeping apostles. On seeing the officers and soldiers "all the disciples forsook him," whilst Jesus, their Master, was led away to the house of the High Priest.

After a long and weary night of accusations and insults Jesus was brought into the Judgment Hall before Pontius Pilate, the Roman Governor of Jerusalem, and accused of blasphemy and sedition.

Pontius Pilate, who had little interest in the religious quarrels of the Jews, examined Jesus to find out whether he was another of the many leaders who roused the people against the Roman rule of Palestine. He found him not guilty of treason, and wished to let him free. But the accusers of Jesus brought other charges against him.

"This Galilean stirs up the people against the Law!" they said.

"If he is a Galilean, then he should be tried before Herod Antipas, Governor of Galilee, and not before me," said Pilate, and sent Jesus to Herod who was then in Jerusalem.

Herod mockingly sent him back to Pilate. And Pilate pronounced sentence over Jesus as finding him guilty of blasphemy, for which crime he was to be punished by death.

It was the custom in those days for the Governor to offer a pardon before the Governor's feast to one prisoner in the land condemned to death. Now there were before Pontius Pilate Jesus of Nazareth and another prisoner, Jesus Bar-Abbas, a man who had stirred up a revolt against the Roman Empire. He was caught and condemned to die.

"For which of these two prisoners do you want my pardon?" Pontius Pilate asked the leaders in the Judgment Hall.

"Bar-Abbas," they replied.

Bar-Abbas was freed, and Jesus of Nazareth was turned over to the soldiers to be put to death in that cruel Roman manner, known as crucifixion.

Guarded by soldiers, and followed by a curious and deriding mob, Jesus and two thieves, who had also been condemned to be crucified that day, were led away from the Judgment Hall to a hill out of town called Golgotha.

It was the custom amongst the Romans then to make the condemned men carry the crosses upon which they were to be executed.

The cross that Jesus bore, so one story tells, was particularly heavy.

During the time that Bar-Abbas stirred up revolt in the city of Jerusalem against the Roman Rule, several people were killed. And one amongst the dead was the only son of a carpenter in Jerusalem.

The father of the dead boy planned to avenge himself for the loss of his only child. But Bar-Abbas had already been arrested, and condemned to death.

The bereaved father went to the Roman soldiers, gave them wine and presents to permit him to make the crosses for the two thieves and Bar-Abbas. And permission was granted him.

He made the cross of Bar-Abbas very heavy so that the condemned rebel would suffer additionally in carrying his cross to Golgotha.

But Bar-Abbas was pardoned, and his cross was given to Jesus of Nazareth to carry.

As Jesus stumbled under the heavy burden, a man named Simon the Cyrene, coming home from work, was drafted by the Roman soldiers to help Jesus carry the cross.

It was customary with the Romans to put an inscription on each cross, giving the name of the crucified and the crime for which he was killed. And over the Cross of Jesus they nailed on the mocking inscription:

JESUS OF NAZARETH
THE
KING OF THE JEWS

When the women of Jerusalem came and offered Jesus a drink made of frankincense, myrrh and vinegar that would lessen his pain, he refused it.

And when the soldiers and the mob derided him, he softly whispered:

"Forgive them, God, for they know not what they do."

But after hours on the cross his pain became unbearable, and Jesus cried out:

"My God, my God, why hast thou forsaken me?"

Then he added in a voice hardly audible:

"It is the end—"

He bowed his head, and gave up the ghost.

9. THE JEWISH SECT CALLED CHRISTIANS

The enemies of Jesus who caused his death were not so much concerned with killing Jesus, as with the desire to destroy the sect he had organized. The death of the leader, they believed, would destroy the sect.

They were mistaken.

The disciples of Jesus gathered secretly, determined to carry on the work of their crucified leader.

They called their dead leader Jesus the Christ, meaning: Jesus the Anointed One. And they called themselves followers of the Christ—CHRISTIANS.

Most of the followers of Jesus were poor people. In Cana and in Capernaum, in Bethsaida and in Gennesaret, in Samaria and in Nain, and later in Bethany and Jerusalem, Jesus was always amongst the lowly, preaching to the poor and the downtrodden.

And amongst the poor and the oppressed the teachings of Jesus flourished after his crucifixion.

Marvelous tales began to be told about Jesus.

It was told that Jesus had turned water into wine at a certain marriage-feast in Cana.

He walked on the sea.

He fed five thousand hungry people with only five loaves of bread.

But most marvelous of all were the stories of his healing powers:

He restored the sight to the blind; and hearing to the deaf; and speech to the dumb.

He made insane, sane again. He made the paralytics walk. He made the lepers whole.

Once, so one story tells, Jesus came by a place called the Pool of Bethesda where many sick people had gathered to bathe, believing its water had healing powers. Amongst the sick was one man who had been lame for thirty and eight years. Jesus turned to this man, and said to him:

"Rise, take up thy bed and walk!"

The man who had not walked for nearly forty years arose from his bed and walked.

Not only did Jesus heal the sick through miracles, but he even brought the dead back to life again.

The marvelous stories about Jesus travelled rapidly amongst the poor of Palestine. And they whispered to each other that Jesus, three days after the crucifixion, rose from his grave and went to Heaven where he will remain until "a time, and times, and half a time" is over. Then he will come and reveal himself to Mankind.

They who were eager for the Coming of the Messiah hoped that the Second Coming of Jesus would be soon, in their own day.

The hope of his immediate Second Coming gained many followers to the new sect who believed that Jesus was *the* Messiah; that Jesus had risen from the dead;

and that his Second Coming was near at hand.

The leaders of the new sect organized their followers into a community, which was called the Community of Goods. All who wished to become members of the sect were first baptized.

They called each other "brother" and "sister."

They ate together.

They cared for the sick and the troubled.

They shunned the rich.

And whatever any one of them had was the property of all.

Such was this early Jewish Sect called Christians.

They gathered in secrecy, and their numbers grew.

When the Rabbis realized that the followers of Jesus were growing in number, they became alarmed and sent out officers to arrest them and put them into prison.

But Rabbi Gamaliel, grandson of Rabbi Hillel the Old whose teachings Jesus admired, saved the leaders of Christianity by saying:

"Refrain from these men and let them alone. If their work and teachings be of men it will come to nought. But if it comes from God, as they claim, you cannot overthrow it."

10.   PAUL OF TARSUS

Long before the days of Jesus, the Jews had begun to be scattered among the nations. At first they were carried away from home by force. Later they left their land of their own free will.

And in the days of Jesus there existed in the city of Tarsus, in Cilicia, a large Jewish community. Amongst them was one, a rich merchant, named Cissai the Benjamite, who had a son named Saul.

Because Saul was born a free Roman citizen, he was also known by his Roman name, Paul. And because he was the only son of a rich man, Paul received a good education.

As a young boy Paul spent much of his time along the water front of Tarsus watching the ships come from over the Great Sea, now called the Mediterranean.

Paul longed to become a sailor. But his father wished his son to become a Rabbi. When Paul was old enough he was sent to Jerusalem to study under Rabbi Gamaliel, grandson of Rabbi Hillel the Old.

And so, whilst Jesus, during his days in Nazareth and Cana, came under the influence of the noble teachings of Rabbi Hillel, Paul of Tarsus in Jerusalem, who was about the same age as Jesus, came under the influence of the gentle Rabbi's grandson.

After Paul's studies were completed he returned to Tarsus, his birthplace, and there he taught the Law and worked with his father.

The news of the crucifixion of Jesus reached Paul in Tarsus. But it did not interest him much. John the Baptist and Jesus of Nazareth were to him only two of many religious leaders who caused their own destruction. Paul had no sympathy with anyone who taught anything that was against the Holy Law.

Like so many Rabbis of his day, Paul believed that with the execution of Jesus, his followers would fall apart.

And like his friends the Pharisees and Rabbis he was mistaken.

Trouble arose in Jerusalem. The followers of Jesus had begun to gather in secrecy to spread the teachings of Jesus. And word was sent to Paul in Tarsus, saying:

"Rabbi Paul, if the Law of Moses and the Mission of Israel are sacred to you, then come to Palestine and help us destroy the Nazarenes, called Christians, whose numbers grow and grow, and whose influence against the Law is becoming felt."

Paul immediately went down to Jerusalem to do what he could to destroy the new sect. He was a shrewd organizer, and he prepared his forces against the scattered followers of Jesus. He persecuted them bitterly in Jerusalem, and followed them to Samaria. When told that their numbers were growing in Damascus, Paul started out on a journey to that city, determined to destroy them.

But on the way to Damascus Paul experienced a change of heart. He continued to Damascus, not to persecute the members of the new sect, but to join them and help them spread their Gospel.

From then on, to the end of his days, Paul devoted himself to the task of spreading the teachings of Jesus.

For twenty-five years he travelled from city to city and from country to country. Wherever Paul came he sought out the scattered synagogues, and there he established himself and preached the Gospel.

Though Paul was not pleasing in appearance, and a

poor speaker, his sincerity gained him large audiences.

That did not mean that he at once made many converts to his teachings. The Jews in the foreign lands scorned him, as Jesus had been scorned in Jerusalem. And the Greeks and Romans, to whom the entire Jewish Religion was strange, would not take his teachings seriously. They considered themselves much superior to the Jews, and paid little attention to the religion of these people from conquered Judea.

Paul was not disheartened by the slowness with which people accepted the Gospel. He travelled to Syria, and to Cilicia, and to Macedonia, and to Crete, and to Sicily, and to Rome in Italy. And wherever he went he carried with him the Glad Tidings, saying:

"This Jesus whom I preach unto you is Christ, Messiah!"

Wherever he went he organized the little groups of followers, and brought news to them from other groups elsewhere, and made them all feel that they were members of a great brotherhood that was to conquer the earth.

And as he travelled about organizing the churches in the name of Jesus, he wrote letters to his followers in the various lands, explaining his Faith, and with these letters strengthened the faith of his organized churches everywhere.

When Paul went to Rome to organize a Christian Church there, he was arrested and charged with treason. For several years he remained in prison. Then he was tried before Emperor Nero and released.

But he continued to preach in Rome. He was arrested again, tried, and put to death.

Paul was dead. But his work was accomplished.

At the time Paul became converted to the teachings of Jesus, the new Jewish sect was very weak.

At the time Paul died, and due to his untiring labors, Christianity was strongly rooted and hoped to become the Religion of the World.

11. THE RISE OF THE NON-JEWISH CHRISTIANS

Paul had begun to spread the Gospel of Jesus amongst the Gentiles outside of Palestine.

After his death the work of the Christians was almost entirely given over to the conversion of the Gentiles, especially the Greeks and the Romans.

For the Greeks and the Romans of that time were ready for a new religion to take the place of their own.

The religion of the Greeks was a religion without a Founder, without Sacred Scriptures, and almost without a Priesthood.

The Greeks believed that their country, Greece, was in the exact center of the earth, and that in the very center of their country there was a very high mountain, called Mount Olympus. On top of that mountain lived the many gods they believed in.

Far away from their country, on the shores of the beautiful river Oceanus, they believed, was a group of marvelous islands, called the Isles of the Blest, where people who led the good life were taken by the gods to enjoy eternal happiness.

Of the many gods the Greeks believed in, Jupiter was King of the Gods. Juno was Queen of Heaven. Apollo was god of the Sun, Medicine, Music, and Poetry. Venus was Goddess of Beauty, Laughter, and Marriage. Neptune was God of the Waters. Pluto was God of Hell.

The gods of the Greeks were almost like people. They fell in love, they hated, they suffered pain, they became angry, they sought pleasure, and they were jealous of each other.

Besides these almost-human gods, the Greeks had half-gods, like Hercules. And they even had ordinary human beings that were worshipped like gods.

In the end there were so many gods, half-gods, and human deities in Greece to believe in, that the people believed in none of them.

Almost the same condition existed amongst the Romans during the days of Paul.

Many of the Greeks and Romans who were eager to find a religion to satisfy them were attracted to the synagogues of the Jews where they listened to the teachings of the One Just God. But the Jews insisted that they who accepted Judaism must follow their Law and customs. And it was very hard for the Greeks and the Romans to accept the Law and all the customs of the Jews.

When Paul came and said that Greeks and Romans could enter the Church without obeying the Jewish Law, as long as they accepted Jesus as their Lord, the newly founded Church gained many followers amongst them.

And so the teachings of Jesus, through the Church

founded by Paul, began to spread amongst the Gentiles.

About a hundred years after the death of Jesus, His teachings began to spread through Asia Minor, Syria, Macedonia, Greece, and Rome. And even in Egypt, Land of the Nile, they began to take root.

In those days the Christians looked upon themselves as a new race on earth, the true Israel, the true Chosen of God.

Each Sunday, which they called the Lord's Day, they met to pray and read the Bible.

Each Wednesday and Friday they fasted.

Daily they repeated a prayer known as the Lord's Prayer.

They were kind to the sick, and generous to the poor. Some of them went so far as to sell themselves into slavery so that, with the money received, they could help those in distress.

About a hundred years after the death of Paul the Sacred Writings of the Christians were gathered into a book. The Christians considered the Old Testament, sacred writings of the Jews, as their Sacred Scriptures. To this they added a small book, called:

The New Testament.

Each man that became a Christian felt that it was his duty to go out and spread the Gospel. Each one considered himself or herself a missionary. In that way the numbers of followers grew from day to day.

In those days the subjects of the Roman Emperor worshipped their king as if he were a god. But the Christians refused to worship him. And for that they were brutally persecuted.

For nearly three hundred years the Christians suffered persecution under the Roman Emperors. But the persecution only drew the Christians together in their faith, and strengthened their belief.

In the year 312 A.D. Constantine, Emperor of Rome, became a Christian and made Christianity the State Religion. That ended the persecution of the Christians.

But as soon as the persecutions ended, quarrels arose amongst the Christians of the various lands. Many sects began to arise, each teaching a different belief in Jesus, or the Apostles.

Some of these sects taught that Jesus was God.

Others taught that Jesus was in every way a human being.

Still others taught that the Bishops of the Church were not as holy as they claimed to be.

But even though they quarrelled amongst themselves and began hating each other, they still continued to spread their teachings amongst the heathen, each sect trying to make as many converts as possible.

About six hundred years after the death of Paul it seemed that Christianity would soon become the religion of all mankind, that it would become the Universal Religion.

But just about that time, towards the beginning of the Seventh Century of the Christian reckoning, a new religion made its appearance in Arabia that soon rivalled Christianity in growth and popularity.

Part Four: MOHAMMEDANISM

FLAMING SWORD OF THE DESERT

Mohammed Said:

"When God created the creation, He wrote a book, which is near Him upon the Heavenly Throne. And in this book it is written:

Verily my love overcometh my anger."

FOUNDED: 622 A.D.

FOUNDER: Mohammed ibn Abdullah (570-632 A.D.)

PLACE: Mecca, Arabia

SACRED BOOKS: *The Koran* (The Reading). The book consists of 114 *surahs* or chapters which present Mohammed's revelations. They are not arranged topically or in the order he received these revelations, but according to length—the shortest coming first and the longest, last.

NUMBER OF ADHERENTS: 322,000,000

DISTRIBUTION: Principally in Arabia, Pakistan, Africa, part of China, Indonesia and Asiatic Russia.

MOHAMMEDANS IN THE UNITED STATES: About 35,000

SECTS: Mohammedanism is known as *Islam,* which means 'Submission.' Those who submit to the teachings of *Islam* are called *Moslems. Moslems* are divided into two major divisions: The *Sunnites* and the *Shi'ites*. Originally the division took place because of the dispute concerning the succession of Mohammed, called the *Caliphate*. Some claimed that the Caliph should be selected; others maintained that the Caliphate should go to the descendants of Mohammed. The two divisions have developed many differences in the practice of Islam, and now have many sects.

MOHAMMEDANISM:

Flaming Sword of the Desert

1. THE LEGEND OF THE SACRED CITY

Long, long ago, so the Arabian story tells, in the days when Abraham, son of Terah, was still alive, he had a wife named Sarah, and another named Hagar. Sarah had a son, and Hagar had a son, and the two wives of Abraham were jealous of each other.

One day Sarah, who was Abraham's favorite wife, said to her husband:

"Abraham, I want you to promise me that my son Isaac shall be your heir and successor."

"It shall be as you say," Abraham promised.

"Hagar despises me, and hopes that her son Ishmael will grow up to be your heir. Promise me to send Hagar and her son away."

Abraham replied:

"I promise!"

The next morning Abraham woke very early and sent Hagar and Ishmael away from home.

Hagar, carrying the small boy on her shoulders, wandered far into the desert near the Red Sea until she became very tired and very thirsty. Hagar seated herself on a rock and wept in fear that she and her child would die of thirst in the desert.

As she sat there weeping, her little boy, Ishmael, kicked the sand in great anger. At the exact spot where he kicked the earth, a spring of fresh water suddenly gushed out of the desert sand.

When Abraham learned of the miracle that had happened to his son Ishmael in the desert, he came to the spring and near it built a temple. In the eastern corner of the temple he set the Black Stone he had inherited from his forefathers and which Adam, the First Man on Earth, had brought with him from the Garden of Eden.

Near that temple, called the *Kaaba*, close to the Spring of Ishmael, called the *Zemzem*, Hagar and her son remained. There Ishmael grew up, and there he raised a large family. And the children and grandchildren of Ishmael built around the Sacred Temple their Sacred City: Mecca.

There is another story that long before Ishmael was born, long before Abraham was born, even 2000 years before the world was created, the *Kaaba* had already been built in Heaven. When Adam the First was driven out of the Garden of Eden for doing something he ought not to have done, he built on earth another *Kaaba* like the one Above, exactly under the heavenly *Kaaba*.

And it was not far from the *Kaaba* Adam built that Ishmael kicked open the *Zemzem*, the Sacred Well. About these two holy places grew up the Sacred City, called Mecca.

The offspring of Ishmael multiplied and began to spread out East, to the Persian Gulf; North, towards the Mediterranean Sea; and South, to the Gulf of Aden. But no matter how far they travelled, and no matter where they settled, Mecca remained to them the Sacred City of their land.

To Mecca, City of God, they came on pilgrimages to worship at the *Kaaba*, to kiss the Black Stone handed down from Adam, and to drink the sacred waters of the Well of Ishmael.

The children of Israel, son of Isaac, son of Abraham, had multiplied into the race called Jews.

The children of Ishmael, son of Hagar and Abraham, multiplied into the race called Arabs.

2.   THE RELIGION OF THE ARABS

Like all people of long ago, the Arabs of long ago were Nature Worshippers.

They worshipped the sun and the stars, and the spirits of the sun and stars. They also worshipped the memory of their forefathers Abraham and Ishmael. And in Mecca, near the Sacred Temple, they set up idols, too, which they worshipped.

They had three hundred and sixty idols, one for each day in their year. (The Arab years has only 360 days.) The most important of these was Habal, an idol made in the form of a man, chiselled out of red agate, with one hand made of gold.

Above all their nature gods, spirits, and idols they worshipped *Allah Taala,* the Most High God. Though they recognized *Allah Taala* as the Most High God, they paid more attention to the stars, and to the idols.

They did not all worship the same idols. Arabia, in those days, was divided into many clans and tribes, and each tribe had idols and beliefs of its own. The tribes often fought each other fiercely and derided each other's beliefs, yet they felt related to each other in their common ancestry.

Because of its geographical position, Arabia was at no time in history oppressed by the great powers of East and West. The ambition of Babylon, Persia, Greece, and Rome never fell too heavily upon the land of the Arabs. Nor have these conquering nations of the past ever brought to Arabia their knowledge and civilization.

Arabia was left alone to its ignorance; to its fierce tribal wars; and to its confusion of religious beliefs. The land teemed with beliefs in Sacred Stones, Sacred Palms, and Sacred Hills.

From time to time rumors spread over the land about the discovery of a hill, or a heap of stones, or a grove of trees that had healing powers or brought good luck. The belief in the power of these sacred places was so great in Arabia that sometimes an Arab would travel for hundreds of miles over the treacherous desert to a newly discovered spot which travellers had reported was sacred.

And all Arabs, everywhere, firmly believed in the holiness of Mecca where were the *Kaaba* and the Well of Ishmael.

Arabia was known as "The Land of Incense," and Mecca was its market-place. On their pilgrimages to the Sacred Temple the Arabs brought along with them incense and spices and perfumes to be sold or exchanged in the market-places of Mecca. In that way they combined Religion with Business.

Naturally, the rich merchants of Mecca profited by the arrival of the stream of pilgrims whose products they bought. And they encouraged the pilgrims to come often to their city, telling them that the trip alone would bring them good luck.

In time the merchants of Mecca claimed that the Well of Ishmael was their private property, and began to sell its waters to the worshippers. But ignorant as the Arabians were, they began to doubt whether there could be any holiness in water sold as merchandise.

"If there is no holiness in the waters of the *Zemzem*," some pilgrims said, "then how much holiness can there be in all those idols and images?"

"Very little!" many thought, though they were silent.

Slowly they lost faith in the powers of the waters of the *Zemzem,* in the holiness of the *Kaaba,* and the divinity of their idols.

With their belief in holy things crumbling, the Arabs turned to gambling, drinking, and fortune-telling.

Had they been highly civilized people in those days, they might have turned to science and invention. But they were ignorant. And nothing stirs the hearts of the ignorant more than the hope of learning what their future holds for them. They think of the future as something hidden in a mysterious place which, if only people could discover the secret, they might be permitted to look into and see all that is going to happen to them. This secret the Arabs attempted to discover through star-gazing; through signs in the air; by dissecting birds and mice; or by walking in circles; or by drawing lots.

The drawing of lots led to gambling.

Gambling led to various degrading practices.

Many Jews, who came to Arabia after the destruction of Jerusalem by the Romans, preached to them the teachings of Judaism. Later Christian Missionaries arrived to spread amongst the Arabs the Gospel of Jesus.

But the Arabs would listen to neither.

They were interested only in their business, horsemanship, poetry-contests, and the pleasures of wine and gambling.

3. SHEPHERD INTO MERCHANT

In the year 570 A.D., when gambling and drunkenness and strange superstitions ruled the minds of the Arabs, a child was born into the home of one of the aristocratic families in Mecca. and he was named Mohammed.

Among the Arabs there are many, many tales of what took place during Mohammed's childhood. There is one story that when Mohammed was born all the idols in the world trembled and tumbled down from their pedestals. And another story tells that when the child Mohammed opened his eyes for the first time, he lifted them towards heaven and exclaimed:

"La ilaha illa Allah, Mohammed rasul Allah!" (There is no god but Allah, and Mohammed is the Prophet of Allah!)

But all we actually know of Mohammed's childhood is that at the age of six he had lost both his father and his mother, and was taken into the home of one of his uncles, Abu Talit.

As soon as Mohammed was old enough to look after a flock of sheep, he was hired out as a shepherd's helper. And out on the edge of the desert Mohammed spent his childhood and early youth, herding sheep to earn his bread and shelter. The desert was his school, and the sun by day and the stars on clear nights were his teachers.

When he grew older Mohammed left the herding of sheep and became a camel-driver. Through the desert he led caravans laden with Arabia's products that were to be sold in the markets of Egypt in the West, Persia in the East, and Syria in the North.

Mohammed's reputation as a caravan leader gained him favor amongst the merchants of Mecca. A wealthy widow, Kadijah by name, employed him through her agents, and Mohammed was sent with a caravan laden with spices and perfumes to Syria, entrusted with the sale of this merchandise and the purchase, in exchange, of silk and linen.

Mohammed returned from the journey in due time, and immediately went to render an account to the widow Kadijah.

Kadijah was forty years old and the mother of three children. But when Mohammed saw her for the first time in her home he was greatly surprised at her youthful appearance and her beauty. Even more surprised was Kadijah at the appearance of Mohammed who had been employed in her services, but whom she now met for the first time.

Though Mohammed was not very tall, he was so broad-shouldered that he appeared like a giant. He had curly black hair and a curly beard, and from between his lips the whiteness of his teeth was dazzling. He came forward to Kadijah with a quick step and bowed graciously.

As soon as Mohammed began to speak, Kadijah was aware that never before had she heard a voice as musical as his. And though Mohammed spoke of merchandise, of sales and profits, and of hardships on the desert, his sentences were as rhythmic as the poems of the famed poet Labid.

Mohammed concluded his account of his first trip as Kadijah's representative, and returned home.

That same afternoon messengers came to him and asked:

"What is it, O Mohammed, that keeps you from marrying?"

"Too poor am I, neighbors!" Mohammed replied. "Not until my fortune is secure will I marry."

"But if a rich and worthy woman sought your hand in marriage, what would be your answer then, O Mohammed?"

"And what might be her name?"

"Kadijah!" the messengers replied.

"Kadijah I would marry whenever she consents!" Mohammed exclaimed happily.

And so, at the age of twenty-five, Mohammed, camel-driver of the deserts of Arabia, married Kadijah, a wealthy widow of Mecca. And through his marriage the poor camel-driver became one of the richest merchants of Mecca.

4. MERCHANT INTO PROPHET

For fifteen years Mohammed lived happily with Kadijah, increased their wealth, and gained the respect of the people of Mecca.

But the thought of the mixed idolatry of his people, and of the great drunkenness and gambling in the land, greatly depressed Mohammed, and he often wondered what could be done to improve the conditions of his countrymen.

As a camel-driver, Mohammed had learned much of the teachings of Judaism and Christianity from the many Jews and Christians he had met and talked with in the market-places of Syria and Persia and Egypt. Mohammed had never learned to read and write, but after his marriage his wife's cousin, Waraka, who had accepted the Jewish Faith, often read the Bible to him.

When the New Testament was read to Mohammed, the story of Jesus convinced him that what his country (Arabia) needed was an inspired prophet and leader who would rouse the Arabs to faith in One God, and who would lead them from their evil practices to the ways of the good life.

The teachings of the Testaments, New and Old, were

now always in Mohammed's mind. Mohammed began leaving the city for the hills surrounding Mecca, and there he spent many hours brooding over the conditions in his country and how they might be changed for the better through prophetic leadership.

One day, as Mohammed sat reflecting on the fate of his people, it seemed to him an angel came and stood before him, and said:

"I am the angel Gabriel!"

Then the angel showed him a golden tablet, and commanded:

"Read!"

"I cannot read!" said Mohammed.

"Read!" the angel commanded again.

And Mohammed who had never learned to read, read:

"O thou who are wrapped, rise up and warn!
And thy Lord magnify,
And thy raiment purify,
And abominations shun,
And grant not favors to gain increase!
And wait for thy Lord!"

This, and more and more was written on the golden tablet in the hands of the angel Gabriel.

When the vision of the angel and the tablet faded away, Mohammed hurried home and told his wife of his strange experience.

Kadijah believed that her husband had actually spoken with an angel, and she encouraged him to go out into the foothills again and await new revelations from Heaven.

Mohammed obeyed her, and again and again he imagined that the angel Gabriel appeared, each time with a new message from Heaven.

Slowly the idea that he was a Prophet chosen by God grew upon Mohammed, and he began to preach to his family and relatives. After gaining several followers amongst his immediate family, Mohammed went out to the Sacred Temple to preach to the people who had gathered to worship the idols.

He arose before them grave and dignified, and slightly trembling with excitement, he began:

"There is no god but Allah, and Mohammed is the Prophet of Allah!"

"What sign have you that there is no god but Allah,

and that you are his Prophet?" many in his audience demanded scornfully.

Mohammed was very sensitive to ridicule, and he blushed in confusion at the question. But he thought it best to continue the message he had brought to the people, and to ignore the scoffers.

Mohammed raised his voice, and in short, rhythmical sentences began to tell the story of their forefather Abraham and how he destroyed the idols in his father's house, in the land of the Chaldees.

"What sign have you that there is no god but Allah and that you are his Prophet?" Mohammed was interrupted again.

Many who were present began to laugh and to shout:

"Give us a sign that there is no God but Allah! Show us a miracle!"

Mohammed's forehead became covered with perspiration, then he answered in an impassioned, fiery voice:

"Ye who seek signs and miracles:

"Behold, it is Allah who raised the heavens without pillars that ye can see; then He ascended the Throne and subdued the sun and the moon;

"And it is He who spread out the earth, and put thereon firm mountains and flowing rivers;

"Ye who seek signs and miracles:

"By the day-break, and by the night that cometh on; by the sun in its rising brightness; by the morning and by the afternoon; by the fig tree and by the olive and the date; verily in that are signs for you to reflect!

"O, unbelievers, I will not worship that which ye worship!

"Say, Allah is One God, and there is not anyone like unto Him!"

5.   THE YEARS OF STRUGGLE

After his first sermon to the people, Mohammed came again and again to preach whenever the spirit moved him. The belief in One God grew within his mind, and he rose before the people near the Sacred Temple and poured his message in burning eloquence into the cold ears of unbelievers. They laughed at him good-humoredly.

"There goes the man who claims to know what goes on in Heaven!" they shouted when they saw him coming.

And when he began to preach, they made sport of him and sang loud, vulgar songs.

Still Mohammed ignored them and went on with his preaching.

As long as Mohammed only urged them to turn from idol-worship to the belief in One God, Allah, the people of Mecca permitted Mohammed to continue preaching. The belief in Allah Taala was not foreign to them. And Mohammed's admonitions about their gambling, drinking, and spending much time in fortune-telling only amused them.

But Mohammed did not stop with attacks on idolatry, drunkenness and gambling. He began to preach against the rich merchants and leaders in Mecca who used the Well of Ishmael and the Temple of the Kaaba as sources of profit. The merchants and rich men who, to that time had ignored Mohammed's sermons, were incensed at such attacks and sent messengers to Mohammed's family warning them to stop Mohammed from preaching any more against the corruption of the rich.

Mohammed, when told about the rich men's warning, replied:

"Not even if you set the sun against me on my right hand, and the moon on my left hand would I leave my mission!"

And he went on preaching.

For years Mohammed persisted in preaching beliefs that were really a mixture of the old beliefs of the Arabs, Judaism, Christianity, and his own ideas of reform. A very small group of followers had attached themselves to him during these years, and these followers he taught his religion which he called ISLAM, meaning: Submission—submission to the commands of Allah.

His followers he called *Moslems,* meaning: True Believers.

The sermons, or speeches, which Mohammed made were written down by one of his followers, Abu Bekr, and these Moslems read wherever they gathered, and with these sermons, which they claimed were revealed to Mohammed by God through the angel Gabriel, they tried to attract followers.

The leaders and rich people of Mecca still watched Mohammed's every step. And as soon as they suspected that the numbers of his followers were increasing, they passed a law that any man who accepted *Islam* should be driven out of Mecca.

Mohammed went on preaching. But people did not want to risk being driven away from their homes, and they dared not accept Mohammed's religion.

Kadijah, Mohammed's ever faithful comforter, died and Mohammed was grief-stricken.

Still he went on preaching.

But depressed by his failure to get the people of his own city to abandon gambling and their other evil ways, Mohammed decided to go to Taif, a city seventy miles away from Mecca, and spread his teachings there.

Taif was the center of a wide grape-country, and the grape-growers and wine merchants hated Mohammed for his teachings against drinking. No sooner had Mohammed begun to preach in their city, than the merchants attacked him and drove him out with stones.

Mohammed returned to Mecca.

And he went on preaching.

One day twelve pilgrims from Yathrib, a city about two hundred and seventy miles away from Mecca, came to Mohammed and asked him to explain his teachings to them. In Yathrib there were many Jews, and from them the pilgrims had heard about their belief in One God and this hatred of idols. When Mohammed preached to these people from Yathrib they could easily understand him.

To them Mohammed said:

"My teachings are simple:
Allah is the One God, and Mohammed is his Prophet;
Give up idolatry;
Do not steal;
Do not lie;
Do not slander;
And never become intoxicated.
If you follow these teachings, then you follow *Islam*."

The next year seventy-five pilgrims from Yathrib came to Mohammed asking him to accept them into his religion.

From amongst these Mohammed chose twelve men, appointed them his Apostles, and told them to return to Yathrib and spread Islam.

The people of Mecca found out that Mohammed was trying to gain a following in Yathrib, and they carefully

worked out a plan to kill him before he had a chance
to spread his teachings any further.

But on the night that they planned to kill him, Mohammed fled from Mecca on his favorite camel, Al Kaswa, and escaped to Yathrib.

That night, on which Mohammed fled to Yathrib, is
the most important date in the religion of *Islam,* and is
now remembered as the *Hegira,* the Night of the Flight.

6. PROPHET INTO RULER

The Christians count time from A.D (*Anno Domini,* the
Year of the Lord) the year Jesus was born in Bethlehem.

But the followers of Islam count time neither from the
day Mohammed was born, nor from the day of his first
vision, nor from the day of his death. They calculate
time from A.H. (*Anno Hegira,* the Year of the Flight),
meaning from the time Mohammed, in his fifty-third year,
ran away from Mecca to join his followers in Yathrib.

And that was really the most important year in the
life of Mohammed and in the history of the religion he
founded.

Up to the time of his flight, Mohammed had been a
Prophet of a new religion. After the Flight he became the
Founder of its Church.

In Mecca Mohammed was scoffed at and persecuted
bitterly. But when he came to Yathrib he was received
with open arms, and proclaimed ruler of the city. Even
the name of the city was changed from Yathrib to *Medina,*
meaning: City of the Prophet. And Medina the city has
remained ever since.

In Medina Mohammed gathered about him his faithful
followers and began to organize his religion. He was no
longer content with reforming only the people of Mecca,
but wished to reform all the people of Arabia.

Though Medina was only half as large as Mecca, it
was a better place for Mohammed to organize his work.
Medina was a walled city surrounded by fruitful date or-
chards. There, Mohammed knew, he could fortify himself and his followers against hunger and against his
enemies.

In Mecca Mohammed had wanted the people to accept
him as the Prophet of Allah. In Medina he planned to
have the people accept him as their uncrowned ruler,

maker of their laws, leader of their armies, and judge of all their affairs.

In order to establish this power he organized an army.

But to keep up an army it is necessary to have food and clothes and money. Where was he to get it?

Mohammed went out to the edge of the desert, wrapped himself up in a number of blankets against the chill of the evening, and meditated. As he sat there thinking of ways to support his army, he heard again the voice of the angel Gabriel, calling.

"O thou who art wrapped up, rise up and warn!"

And Mohammed returned to his followers and told them that the Angel of God had come to him and instructed him to go out and waylay the caravans carrying goods from Mecca to foreign lands.

Mohammed had spent many years as a camel-driver in the desert, and he knew the paths of the caravans, as well as the passes where they could be most easily attacked.

Mohammed and his followers went out plundering caravans. And whatever they plundered was divided equally amongst them. The success of their attacks on the caravans, Mohammed explained to his followers, proved that Allah was with them.

Mohammed had organized these pillages to support his army. But he also wanted the robberies to incite the merchants of Mecca, and bring them out into open battle.

His plan succeeded.

After many of their caravans had been robbed, the Meccans gathered to decide what to do.

"It is no longer safe for us to send our merchandise to foreign markets," they said, "and all because of Mohammed."

"Let us declare war upon him," one merchant suggested.

"He is in Yathrib and we are in Mecca, nearly one hundred leagues away. How can we reach him?"

"Let us hire soldiers and go up to Yathrib, and destroy him and his followers to the last man!" suggested the merchant.

His advice was taken.

Soldiers were hired. Spears were given them to fight with. And camels were provided for them to travel on, fast dromedaries that could pursue the enemy and overtake him.

War was declared on Yathrib, called Medina, and on Mohammed its ruler, and on all the people who followed him.

Mohammed had learned of the plan of the Meccans to attack him, and he quickly organized his forces to meet their army.

In one of the battles with the Meccans Mohammed almost lost his life. The Meccans, that day, succeeded in breaking through his ranks and put the Moslems to flight.

"Return and fight!" Mohammed shouted to his men. "The Prophet of God is here and does not flee! Come back!"

He was not heeded. His soldiers fled, leaving their leader almost entirely unprotected. A volley of stones and arrows began flying in Mohammed's direction from the Meccan soldiers who had recognized him. A Meccan soldier on horseback rushed up to Mohammed and swung his sword at his head.

Just at that moment one of Mohammed's faithful servants, who had not deserted his Master, jumped forward and raised his hand. The blow of the sword cut the servant's arm from his body. But Mohammed was saved.

The Meccans believed that Mohammed had been killed, and they returned home singing their victory.

Their joy did not last long. Their caravans were plundered again, and Mohammed, whom they believed to be dead, was organizing a large army for new wars with his enemies. The enraged Meccans went to war again. But victory was on the side of Mohammed who had skilfully organized his army.

And with every success in battle, the faith of Mohammed's followers increased.

When the wars with Mecca were over, Mohammed settled in Medina to further the spreading of his religion.

Though fame and power were his, Mohammed remained unchanged by his success. At home he was soft-spoken and gentle. He treated his servants as if they were his own children. At the door of his house he ordered a bench to be placed, and whosoever came and sat upon it was given food and clothing. He loved children and was never too busy to stop and play with them. And when he and his men were out in the battle field, though he was their Prophet and their Leader, he insisted upon doing his share of the work.

But in war as in peace he went on preaching to his followers. He tried to make his teachings so simple that even the most ignorant could understand and follow them. In order to be a good Moslem, a True Believer, he preached, there are only Five Important Rules to follow:

Believe in Allah, and Mohammed, His Prophet;

Pray five times each day;

Be kind to the poor and give alms;

Keep the Fasts during the Month of Fasts;

And make the yearly pilgrimage to Mecca, the Holy City.

7. THE CONQUEST OF MECCA

Amongst the most important commandments of his religion, Mohammed placed the Pilgrimage to Mecca. He knew that for centuries his people had considered the Temple of the Black Stone and the Well of Ishmael, in Mecca, sacred, and that it would please them to continue to keep those places as holy.

Besides, in his plans to conquer Mecca he wished to make it a religious duty for him and his followers to enter the Sacred City.

"What if the Meccans will not permit us to enter and worship in their city?" Mohammed was asked by his followers.

"I, last of the Prophets, am sent with the sword! The sword is the key to heaven and hell; all who draw it in the cause of the Faith will be rewarded!" Mohammed replied.

Eight years after his flight from his birthplace, Mohammed gathered an army of 10,000 armed followers, and marched down to Mecca.

When the news of the approaching army became known to the people of the city, they fled into the hills in terror. Mecca was deserted by all its inhabitants. And from the surrounding hilltops the people watched in awe the approach of the great army come from Medina.

With their Prophet and Leader at their head, riding his favorite camel Al Kaswa, the army entered the deserted city.

They marched through the empty streets directly to the Sacred Temple.

Mohammed stopped his camel before the haughty

statue of the idol Habal with the golden hand, and point-
ing at it with his staff, he said:

"Truth is come, and falsehood is fled away!"

At once his followers tore the idol down and smashed
it into pieces.

Mohammed then drove up to the next idol, pointed his
staff, and repeated:

"Truth is come, and falsehood is fled away!"

And his followers destroyed it also.

So he went from idol to idol, until every one of the
three hundred and sixty idols was demolished.

Mohammed then ordered his men not to destroy anything in the city, nor to plunder its markets, nor to commit any wrong.

When the people who had fled into the hills came back
again and saw that Mohammed had come peacefully to
worship at the Sacred Temple, and was not intent upon
murder and robbery, they accepted his teachings, *Islam,*
and acknowledged Mohammed as their Prophet and
Leader.

8. THE LAST WORDS OF THE PROPHET

Mohammed was beginning to grow old. The blood in his
veins had thickened. His walk was no longer bold. His
sight began to fail him. And he was growing slow of
movement. But his ambitions did not diminish. As acknowledged leader and Prophet of Arabia, he began to
dream of a World Empire ruled by Islam.

With the same energy that he organized his forces in
Medina he began to organize his missionaries to spread
his teachings in foreign lands. He even sent a message to
the Emperor of Rome, saying:

"In the name of God, the Merciful, the Compassionate,
Mohammed, who is the servant of God,
To Heraclitus, the Emperor of Rome,
Peace be on whosoever has gone on the straight road!
After this I say:
Verily I call you to Islam!
Embrace Islam, and God will reward you twofold.
But if you refuse, O ye people of the Book, Beware!
We are Moslems and our religion is Islam!"

To those who were ready to accept Islam peacefully, he sent his blessings. And to those who rejected him, Mohammed sent word, saying:

"I, last of the Prophets, am sent with a sword! The sword is the key to heaven and hell; all who draw it in the name of the Faith will be rewarded!"

His armies swept through the surrounding country, and within three years Mohammed had under his rule all of Arabia and many neighboring tribes.

At the age of sixty-three Mohammed felt that his end was near. He called his followers together and delivered to them his last message.

In this message he repeated what he had often told them before about:

Keeping the Faith as is the will of Allah;

Being kind to the poor;

Giving the laborer his wage before his perspiration is dry;

Not to obey anything that is against the Faith, for "There is no obedience due to sinful commands!"

Nor ever to worship idols.

He ended his message, saying:

"Ye people, harken to my words, for I know not whether after this year I shall ever be amongst you here again:

"Remember that the Faith is of the heart! A keeper of fasts who does not abandon lying and slandering, God careth not about his leaving off eating and drinking!

"Ye people, harken unto my speech, and comprehend it:

"Know that every true believer in the Faith is the brother of every other true believer. All of you are of the same equality: You are all of one brotherhood!"

Three months later Mohammed died.

Many of his followers refused to believe that their Prophet was dead, until Abu Bekr, Mohammed's favorite friend and follower, appeared, and said:

"He who worships Mohammed, let him know that Mohammed is dead; but he who worships Allah, let him know that Allah lives and will not die."

Then the people believed that their Prophet Mohammed had passed away, leaving to them his teachings of the True Belief in Allah, the Most High.

9.   MIRACLES AND WONDERS

After the death of all the great religious leaders of the past their followers related wondrous miracles about them.

There are the *Jatakas,* the birth-legends, of the Buddha. There are the tales of miracles about the birth, life, and death of Moses, Zoroaster, and Jesus.

But about none of the religious leaders of the past are there so many legends of miraculous happenings as about Mohammed. In Arabia, in Persia, in China, and in every land where Mohammed's teachings have followers there are books of legends about the Founder of Islam. Most of the legends are about the birth and infancy of Mohammed.

There is one story that the King and Ministers of Persia were out one night studying the starlit sky, when suddenly there appeared a single star so bright that it rivalled the sun with its light. The King and Ministers looked at each other in wonder, and said:

"Not otherwise, but that a great Prophet has been born!"

When they looked again, they saw that the new star was in the direction of Mecca.

That happened at the hour Mohammed was born.

And when Mohammed was born, another story tells, the mountains began to dance and sing:

"There is no god but Allah!"

The trees whispered happily to each other:

"And Mohammed is his Prophet!"

All the birds that fly gathered around Mecca to sing their praise of Allah. And all the creatures that swim raised their heads above water and exclaimed:

"The time has arrived! Now the world has a light to lead it!"

Even the monstrous fish Tamoosa was very happy.

Tamoosa, as is well known, is the king of all creatures that swim in the seas. Tamoosa has seven hundred thousand tails, and his back is so enormous that seven hundred thousand bullocks with golden horns run around upon it and he does not even feel them.

When Mohammed was born, Tamoosa began to splash the sea with all his seven hundred thousand tails, and nearly overturned the earth in his great joy. And that he might have done, had not Allah quieted Tamoosa in time!

When Mohammed was an infant, many visitors came to see him. But when his face was unveiled, the people had to cover their eyes quickly to avoid being blinded by the brightness that shone from the face of the child.

And seven thousand angels, disguised as little boys and girls, came to Mohammed's home, bringing with them a golden vessel filled with Heavenly Dew. In this vessel the child Mohammed was bathed. That was why he was always clean. When he awoke each morning, his face was clean as if it had just been washed, and his hair was combed and in order.

Later, when Mohammed was a shepherd and a camel-driver in the desert, he never suffered from the heat, because a little cloud always hung low to cast a shadow to protect him wherever he went during the heat of the day.

At night Mohammed's eyes were like to searchlights. When anything was dropped in the dark, Mohammed could bend down and pick it up as easily as if the sun had shone upon that spot.

Once Mohammed and his followers were in the desert. When night came Mohammed, who was very modest, would not undress in the presence of his men. He arose and looked around. Far to the north he could see a tree. And far to the south he saw another. Mohammed called the two trees and they came near and formed a screen between him and his followers.

After conquering Mecca, Mohammed was presented with a bow upon which an eagle had been painted. Mohammed, who preached against all idols, images, and pictures, did not wish to take the picture into his house. But he did wish to keep the present that had been given him. So he placed his hand upon the bow, and immediately the eagle came to life and flew away, leaving the bow clean for Mohammed to keep.

When Mohammed died, his bed was moved aside, and his grave dug exactly underneath the spot where he died. As the gravediggers dug deep into the ground, they found a stone whose radiance could be seen from a very great distance. This stone was placed on Mohammed's grave.

These stories, and thousands of stories like these, are told lovingly about Mohammed by followers of Islam, also called: MOHAMMEDANISM.

10. THE GROWTH OF ISLAM

When Mohammed was born, Arabia was full of idols, star-gazers, soothsayers, fortune-tellers, and fakirs of every kind.

When Mohammed died, idolatry had been rooted out of the land, and the belief in One God was planted firmly in the hearts of the people. The drunkenness and gambling that were popular when Mohammed was young, were banished by his teachings during the short time of his rule.

To his followers after his death, Mohammed left his speeches, or sermons, which were written down by the faithful Abu Bekr, and gathered into a book, called *The Koran,* meaning: The Reading.

The Koran became the Sacred Scriptures of Islam.

Immediately after Mohammed's death, Abu Bekr became the successor to the Prophet. He was called *Caliph,* which means: The Shadow of God on Earth.

Caliph Abu Bekr sent armies to Syria and to Persia and to North Africa to spread Islam.

And when Abu Bekr died, his successors continued the Holy Wars, spreading the Gospel of Mohammed.

Before a hundred years after Mohammed's death were over the religion he founded had conquered Syria in the north, and from there it travelled to Egypt in the west. From Egypt it travelled to Tunis, Tripoli, and Algeria. It came to Persia, to India and China. And it made its way to Europe and reached Spain.

The spread of Islam continued for many, many years. And though in Europe it was stopped by fierce wars against it, it still spreads now in Africa, and in the tropical countries.

As long as Islam remained in Arabia among the Arabs it was a unified religion. But when it began to spread beyond Arabia and brought under its rule different people like the Negroes, Kurds, Caucasians, Mongols, Chinese, and Hindus, various sects began to arise.

Today there are over one hundred and fifty sects of Islam.

The number of True Believers, Moslems, in the various sects are estimated to be over 300,000,000, or a little over one-seventh of the entire population of the world. And, next to Christianity, it is the most active, most growing, and most important religion in existence.

The various sects of Islam have many differing beliefs.
But the most important Articles of Faith are the same
amongst all of them. These important beliefs are:

The Belief in One God, Allah, who rules the world.

The Belief in Angels who do Allah's bidding.

The Belief in Spirits and Devils, who are as numerous
as the angels.

The Belief in the Major and Minor Prophets. Amongst
the Major Prophets they number Adam, Noah, Abraham,
Moses, and Jesus. But the greatest of them all is, of
course, Mohammed.

The Belief in the Day of Judgment. On that day the
True Believers will go to Heaven, which is "a garden of
delight." But they who are not Moslems will go down to
the tortures of the Seven Terrible Hells.

The Belief in Predestination. By "predestination" they
mean that everything in the world that happens, happens
because Allah, the One God, wants it to happen so. A
man cannot choose to do as he wishes. A man could tie
his dog with a thousand ropes, but if Allah has destined
that dog to be free, he would be free.

About this belief in *predestination* many long and difficult books have been written.

But the followers of Mohammedanism, the great number of people, do not worry about the theories explained
in the many serious books. They follow the simple beliefs of their Prophet, and the many customs that go with
his religion.

When they go out into the streets they take their rosaries along with them. These rosaries are, usually, of
ninety-nine beads for the Ninety-Nine Most Beautiful
Names of God. And as they walk, they slip the rosary
through their fingers, murmuring a name for each bead.
If they forget one name in the right order they are not
disturbed, but murmur instead:

Allah, Allah, Allah!

Part Five: THE REFORMATION

OUT OF THE DARK AGES

> *"No one can command or ought to command, or by force compel any man's belief,"* said Luther.

PROTESTANTISM

Protestantism began with the Reformation in Western Europe; but the term was not officially used until 1783, when the Anglicans in the United States called themselves *The Protestant Episcopal Church.*

Today almost all denominations that are not Roman Catholic or Greek Orthodox are designated as Protestants. There are about 250 Protestant denominations or sects. Some are very orthodox, and differ from the Catholics only in that they do not accept the authority of the Pope in Rome; others differ greatly in doctrinal matters.

There are about 800,000,000 Christians in the world today. Of these about 470 million are Catholic, 128 million are Greek Orthodox, and 202 million are Protestants.

In the United States Protestants represent two-thirds of all Christians, and practically every denomination is represented. The three largest Protestant denominations, in numbers of adherents, are: Baptists (over 18 million members); Methodists (over 11½ million members); and Lutherans (nearly 7 million members).

THE REFORMATION:

Out of the Dark Ages

1. EAST IS EAST AND WEST IS ROME

When Constantine, the Augustus, proclaimed Christianity as the State Religion of the Roman Empire, over 1600 years ago, he really offered to combine the Church ideals about the Kingdom of Heaven with the Roman ideals about the Kingdom on Earth.

The Roman Empire, in those days, had under its control almost all the civilized world. Its ideal was to extend its power the world over to rule the *civil* affairs of all mankind. The ideal of the Church was to convert all people in the world to Christianity and govern their *spiritual* affairs.

When the Church and the State were wedded by Constantine, they were really united to rule *all* the affairs of men, both civil and religious.

Through this union of Church and State the Great Roman Empire became: *The Holy Roman Empire.*

At that time the Church was ruled by many Bishops under five Fathers who were known as *Patriarchs* (from the Greek word meaning Fathers). They were also called *Popes* (from the Latin word meaning Fathers).

The most important of these Fathers were the Pope of Rome in the West and the Pope of Constantinople in the East.

From the very beginning the Church of the East differed from the Church of the West, and the Pope of Rome was not at peace with the Pope of Constantinople.

Christians everywhere began to think of Rome as holy ground because Paul and Peter, as well as many of the early Christians, had died there as martyrs. And because of that the Pope of Rome considered himself the highest authority of the Church.

But Constantinople was then the seat of the Great Roman Empire, and the Emperors looked upon Constantinople as also the seat of the Church and the place of highest authority.

So the Pope of Rome and the Pope of Constantinople were jealous of each other.

There was another very important difference between the East and the West: In the East Greek was spoken; and in the West, Latin.

Often, when translations were made from the original Greek into Latin, the meaning of religious words slightly changed. And the beliefs and practices also changed. That caused much unfriendly discussion between the Church of the East and the Church of the West.

As time went on, the differences between the Churches of East and West became greater and greater. And the jealousy between the Popes of Rome and Constantinople grew from day to day.

Then arose a great dispute about Idol-Worship:

The early Christians, who were Jews, and those immediately after them, who were Gentiles, forbade the worship and use of images of any kind in the Church. But in time the Christians East and West began to make images.

They made statues and paintings of the Martyrs, of the Saints, of the Apostles, of Mary, and of Jesus. Some even tried to make images of God. In the West they made, mostly, statues; in the East they made, mostly, painted and gilded images.

These painted and gilded images were called by their Greek name, *ikons*. (Eikon, in Greek, means Image.)

The Christians came and kneeled before these images of stone and painted wood, and prayed to them, and believed that they had great powers.

The Jews, and later the Mohammedans, began to scoff at the Christians, and said:

"Look at those images, at those *ikons!* They have eyes that cannot see; they have ears that cannot hear; they have hands that cannot stir; they have feet that cannot move! Yet these the Christians worship, and then they tell us that their religion is better than ours!"

The clergy of both East and West realized the dangers of idolatry in the Church, but the clergy of the East were powerless before the will of the Emperors and their wives who wished to have the images in the Church. And a great dispute arose.

These differences, and many others, gradually divided the Church of the East from the Church of the West.

During this time Europe was overrun by hordes of barbarians, Goths and Huns and Gauls and Danes and Franks, who established what were later to become the

Kingdoms of England, France, Spain, and Germany. Under the Pope of Rome these barbarians were converted to Christianity, and added greatly to the power of the Western Church.

But whilst the strength of the Western Church flourished, the Roman Empire in the East began to crumble. And the gulf between East and West became wider and wider.

In the year 1054 there came a final break between Rome and Constantinople, and the Church became divided into:

The Greek Orthodox Church in the East; and
The Roman Catholic Church in the West.

2. THE HOLY CRUSADES

Long before the break in the Church took place, as we have seen, there arose the Flaming Sword of the Desert, Mohammedanism, and it sent its armies out over the earth to convert all people to the belief in Allah and Mohammed his Prophet.

Into the hands of Mohammedanism fell Jerusalem, the city sacred to the Christians, for there Jesus had often preached; and there Jesus was crucified.

Rumors began to spread that the Mohammedans had desecrated all the landmarks in Jerusalem sacred to the Christians.

One man, known to us as Peter the Hermit, began to rouse the people of France to gather into crusading armies to conquer Jerusalem for the glory of the Faith. Those who enlisted in the army of the Crusades were offered forgiveness of all their sins.

Thousands of sinners who sought forgiveness, and thousands of believers who were eager to destroy the Mohammedans, and thousands of men who were eager for adventure, and thousands of barbarians who loved to go to war, joined in the Crusades and marched to Jerusalem.

There were several Crusades during the 12th and 13th Centuries, and Jerusalem was conquered and held as a Christian State for some years.

The worst sufferers of these Crusades, however, were not the Mohammedans, but the Christians of the East.

Thousands of Crusaders on the way to Jerusalem swooped down upon their land and demanded to be fed and housed. And they even tried to supplant the Greek Orthodox Church in Constantinople with the Roman Catholic Church.

Some of the leaders of the Greek Orthodox Church suspected that the Crusades were organized not so much against the Mohammedans in Jerusalem, as against the Christians of the East who had broken away from the Roman Church.

But the Crusades failed to conquer the Mohammedans whom they had started out to conquer. And they failed to subjugate the Greek Orthodox Church.

What they did succeed in doing was to create such great evils that, some people believe, we suffer from their effects to this very day. (As an outcome of the Crusades arose an evil known as *Indulgences,* and this led to very important results, as we shall see a little later in this chapter.)

The Crusades completed the break between the Church of the East and the Church of the West. Many times since, attempts have been made to unite the Greek Orthodox Church with the Roman Church, but to this day they stand divided.

3. THE POWER OF ROME

Meanwhile the dominion of the Church of Rome became greater and greater. It controlled almost all of Europe; and missionaries were sent out to the east and to the west and to the north and to the south to convert mankind to Christianity.

And the power of the Pope of Rome grew and grew.

To disobey the Pope's command was considered not only a soul-destroying sin, but also an offense against the government.

In his person the Pope combined all the powers of Heaven and Earth. Not only was he called the Vicar of Christ, but he was also known as:

Prince over all the Nations and Kingdoms.

When a Pope died, another was elected, the way we elect our President. The difference was, of course, that the Popes were not elected by all the people, but by a group of cardinals, called the College of Cardinals.

There was also another very important difference between the election of a Pope and our election of a President: The Pope, as soon as he was elected, could make any law he wished, and the people had to obey it.

One of these laws made by the Pope was that the people had to pay to the Church a portion of all their earnings. We call that taxes.

More than that, the Pope could decide what people should read and what they should not read; what people might study and what they might not study. And whatever the Pope decided was LAW.

What happens to people who disobey the Law? They are punished.

And so the Church punished all people who disobeyed the commands of the Pope and his Cardinals and Bishops.

Some people did not think they ought to pay the taxes the Pope demanded; and some people wished to decide for themselves what books to read; and some people wished to study some of the subjects the Pope prohibited; and some people did not wish to keep all the holidays the Church proclaimed.

These people, when they were caught, were brought before a tribunal and tried. And, if found guilty, they were severely punished.

The more the people were punished, the greater became the number of those who objected to some of the rules of the Church.

And the more people revolted against the rule of the Church, the severer became the punishment.

Then, about the 13th Century, the Church of Rome set up what is known in history as *The Inquisition*.

The Inquisition was a new method of converting people to Christianity. If men or women or children refused to accept Christianity, they were tortured until they died.

Even the early Christians, before Constantine, who were tortured and killed and fed to the lions in Rome, and who are known to us as Martyrs, were not treated more cruelly than the non-Christians during the Inquisition.

The Inquisition lasted over two hundred years, and thousands of people were killed by its orders in the most barbarous manner. People were burned alive on a slow fire, or they were crushed to death by heavy weights, or they were torn to pieces by cruel instruments.

The cruel treatment of the Inquisition was not reserved for Jews and heathens only. It was also directed against Christians, no matter how pious, who dared utter a word against the Rule of the Pope, or dared believe anything the Church did not sanction.

Some brave Christians wrote books against the cruelty of the Inquisition and the despotic power of the Pope. These people were caught and tortured to death in the Inquisition torture-chambers.

But there were people then, as there always are, who were ready to die for the truth. And such people arose in the name of Humanity to protest against the Inquisition, even though threatened with death.

The Inquisition, like the Crusades, started out against the non-Christians, and ended in the persecution of their own brethren.

But the Voice of Justice was not stilled. The power of the truth in protest of the men slain was greater than the power of the sword that killed them.

The more cruel the methods of the Inquisition became, the greater became the number of those who protested against it.

Such were the conditions in Europe towards the end of the 15th Century, when Martin Luther was born in Germany.

4. MARTIN LUTHER

Martin Luther was the son of Hans and Margarete Luther, poor peasants of Eisleben, Germany. Though the Luthers were poor people and had six other children, they gave Martin a good education.

When Martin was old enough, it became his ambition to go through college. His parents did not have the means to help him through a college course, and Martin tried to make his way through a Law School by singing in the streets for his meals and needs. Many students in Germany, in those days, supported themselves in that way. People knew that these were not beggars but hungry students, and now at one door, and now at another a woman would appear and call the singer into the house for a meal.

Martin had almost completed his course of Law, when a very dear friend of his died. The sudden death of one so dear to him made a very strong impression upon young Luther. He immediately gave up his Law course and began to study religion.

He entered a Monastery, and two years later he was ordained into the Priesthood.

In the Monastery Martin Luther's quick intelligence and

learning brought him to the attention of his superiors, and at the early age of twenty-five he was appointed Professor of Philosophy at the University of Wittenberg.

He taught at the University. He preached in the church he was given. And he still found enough time to study the organization of the Christian Church, its history, and its rule.

Though he was a very devout Roman Catholic, there were many things about the behavior and rule of the Pope and the clergy that seemed wrong to Luther. He particularly objected to the Inquisition as being Un-Christian and evil.

"No man can command or ought to command, or by force compel any man's belief," he said.

He could not understand how the Pope or any of his followers hoped to force a man to accept Christianity as they taught it, if he did not accept it in his heart first.

Several years later, Luther and another monk were sent to Rome on a mission. When Luther came in sight of Rome, he fell upon his knees and exclaimed:

"Hail to thee, Holy Rome! Thrice holy for the blood of martyrs shed here!"

It was not long though before Luther realized that Rome was not the holy city he had expected.

He learned that the people of Rome lived shameful lives, and when a man claimed to be a good Christian they called him a fool.

Martin Luther's greatest disappointment came when he reached the dwelling of the Pope. Pope Julius II lived in a castle, surrounded by wealth and served as a King. People came to him and kissed his feet and begged favors. And the Pope, God's representative on earth, sold his grace for a price.

Luther returned to Wittenberg a very unhappy man. His experiences in Rome had convinced him that the entire government of the Pope was somehow wrong, but he did not yet know how the rule of the Pope could be changed for the better. That good Christians could live the good life without the aid of the Pope in Rome had as yet not occurred to Luther.

Several years after Luther returned from Rome Pope Julius II died, and Pope Leo X came into power.

The new Pope, who wished to outdo all the Popes that

had come before him, decided to build a church the like of which had never been built before.

In order to raise money for the great church, to be called St. Peter's Dome, Pope Leo sent out his agents to sell *Indulgences* all over the Christian world.

The Pope and his clergy had a complete list of all the sins a man might commit, and the punishment for each sin. There were some sins for which the sinner could obtain forgiveness through repentance. But there were other sins for which the sinner had to suffer damnation.

During the Crusades complete forgiveness of all sins was promised to those who were ready to sacrifice their lives in a war for the Faith. After the Crusades, a sacrifice in money paid into the Pope's treasury began to be considered a substitute. This payment of money to the Pope to have their sins forgiven by the Lord was known as buying *Indulgences*.

These indulgences were sold wherever there were Christians. And, of course, the greatest sinners were the best buyers.

Not only did the clergy sell indulgences, but even private tradesmen dealt in them, and received a commission of thirty-three and a third per cent. Indulgences, which really mean the Mercy of the Lord, were dealt in as people nowadays deal in stocks and bonds.

To Luther all this merchandising of the Forgiveness of the Lord seemed wrong. He could not understand how it was possible for a man to kill another, then buy for a certain sum of money indulgences from the Pope's agents or a broker, and in that way become innocent before the Lord.

When Pope Leo X sent out his men to sell indulgences in order to raise money for St. Peter's Dome, Luther wrote a number of letters to priests in Germany asking them to protest against the business of indulgences. But these priests were afraid to interfere with the work of the Pope. They knew the power and cruelty of the Inquisition.

Just then Johann Tetzel, representative of the Pope in Germany, arrived to begin the auction of indulgences.

5.   THE PEN THAT TILTED A CROWN

On the night of October 30, 1517, Prince Frederick of Saxony dreamt that he saw a monk come up to a church and write upon its door. The words this monk wrote were so long that they could be seen six leagues away. And the pen he wrote with was so large that it reached from Germany to Rome.

As the monk of Frederick's dream moved his pen, it brushed against the head of the Pope in Rome and almost threw off his crown.

That was a strange dream for Prince Frederick to dream.

But the very next day, October 31, 1517, Martin Luther appeared before the Castle Church of Wittenberg and nailed upon its wooden door a long inscription in Latin.

People passing by near the church stopped to read the notice in which Luther denounced the sale of indulgences. The news was soon carried all over town and a crowd gathered about the church.

Without Luther's knowledge, his challenge was translated from Latin into German. From German it was translated into other European languages. Before four weeks were over it was known all over Germany and all over Europe.

The news reached the Pope, but he only said:

"A drunken German wrote it. When he is sober he will think differently."

But the sale of indulgences fell off rapidly.

The angered Pope then issued an order, called a Papal Bull, to throw Luther out of the clergy and to prohibit any man from reading Luther's writings, or from having anything to do with him. A copy of this order was sent to Luther.

When the order reached Luther he burned it in public.

That marked the final break between Luther and the Church of Rome.

Luther had many admirers and followers who agreed with him in his criticism of the power of the Pope, and they encouraged him to go on with his attacks.

Luther did not disappoint them. He lectured and wrote many books on the subject of the power of the Pope.

In one of these he wrote:

"The Church of Rome, formerly the most holy of all churches, has become the most lawless den of thieves, the very kingdom of sin, death, and hell."

Martin Luther was a tireless worker. During his lifetime he wrote over four hundred books and pamphlets. He translated the Bible into German, and to this day his translation is used in Germany as the King James Version of the Bible is used amongst English speaking people. And he found enough time to preach, and to organize the churches that broke away from the Church of Rome.

Before he died, his teachings called *Lutheranism,* spread over Germany, Norway, Sweden, and Denmark.

The churches organized by him became known as the *Protestant Churches*.

And so the dream of Prince Frederick almost came true.

6.   BEFORE MARTIN LUTHER AND SINCE

Martin Luther was not the first swallow in Church History to bring the summer of the Reformation.

Long before Luther's break with the Pope many conditions arose to make a change in the Roman Catholic Church necessary, and many were the people who championed the need of a change.

The 14th and 15th Centuries are noted for a great awakening from what is known to us as the Dark Ages.

This awakening is called the *Renaissance*.

During these two centuries the great universities of Heidelberg, Cologne, Prague, Vienna and Eufurt were established. And in these universities the New Learning flourished.

During the Dark Ages the Popes forbade the study of Greek and Hebrew, they forbade the study of Greek Philosophy, and the study of classical mythology. But during the 14th and 15th Centuries these studies were revived in the great universities, and the great teachings and literature of the past came to life again.

With the study of Greek and Greek History, a new interest in Art arose. That encouraged the growth of a great art in Europe. During this time the great Leonardo da Vinci painted frescoes that we still treasure; Raphael painted his famous paintings; and Michael Angelo swung his mallet to leave to the world a heritage in carved stone.

Whilst the New Learning rumbled like thunder, and the great masters of brush and chisel were hard at work, the news spread from land to land that Diaz, Vasco da Gama, and Columbus had discovered the shores of a New World, and a route to India by water.

The marvelous discoveries of a new route to India and an unknown continent had not yet been fully told, when the great Polish physician and scientist, Jan Copernicus, made his appearance with a few little instruments under his arm and a small book which he had written to prove his discoveries of the heavens.

Up to that time people believed that the Earth was the center of the universe and that the sun and the moon and stars revolved around the Earth to serve it. (People call that the *Geocentric Theory*.)

Jan Copernicus proved that that was not true. He proved that the earth and the moon and the stars revolve around the Sun and that the Sun is the center of the universe. (This is called the *Heliocentric Theory*.)

From having the most important place in the universe, the earth suddenly dwarfed into an insignificant speck in space, one of many others, revolving around the sun.

Copernicus' startling theory about the universe made people gasp. And it made them think.

In England and in France and in Italy and in Germany and all over the civilized world the bright dawn of the Renaissance stirred people to thought and action.

The great poets and the great writers of those days readily enlisted in a courageous army to advance the New Learning.

At the beginning of the 14th Century the famous poet Dante published a long poem called *The Divine Comedy,* in which the poet describes an imaginary trip through Purgatory, Hell, and Heaven. The guide that leads Dante through Hell and Heaven is not an Angel, nor an Apostle, nor a Saint, but Virgil, a great poet, a heathen.

To us this may not seem very heretical, but in the days of Dante to have shown such great respect for a Roman poet was a crime for which some people were burned at the stake.

After Dante, other great writers began to praise the philosophy of the Greeks, and their mythology, and their great literature.

With all these new ideas coming to life, a change in the religious beliefs and a decline of the power of the Popes was inevitable.

Everywhere, all over Europe, religious reformers arose.

The first important preacher of Reform was a French merchant named

PETER WALDO

Peter Waldo, who lived towards the end of the 12th Century, was a very religious wealthy merchant who undertook the translation of the Holy Scriptures into French. During his studies of the Scriptures he became convinced that the Pope and his followers were not living according to the teachings of Jesus. His own life as a wealthy merchant, he realized, was also not in accord with the teachings of the Gospel.

Peter Waldo gave his wealth away to the poor, and began to preach the teachings of Jesus as he found them in the New Testament.

His sermons attracted a number of people who became his followers, and called themselves *Waldenses*.

When Peter Waldo died, his followers carried on his work and tried to spread his teachings. But the Pope prohibited them from preaching and ordered that the Waldenses should be persecuted and killed wherever found.

But the Waldenses did not stop from spreading their conviction that no one can live the life of a good Christian in luxury and corruption.

The Waldenses, followers of Peter Waldo, preached reform in France. And in England

JOHN WYCLIFF

John Wycliff, a professor at Oxford during the 14th Century, arose as an opponent to the Pope's power over England. John Wycliff denied the absolute infallibility of the Popes, and he criticized many of their practices.

John Wycliff also objected to the sermons and services of the Church in Latin, a language not understood by most people in England. He organized a number of priests and sent them out to preach in English. With the help of some of his friends, Wycliff translated the Bible into English so that all people could read it and understand it.

Though Wycliff's work was suppressed in his own country, it found many followers outside of England. It reached Germany and Bohemia and it influenced the thinking of many young reformers.

Then Luther came and started the organization of the Protestant Churches.

And at the same time the revolt against the Roman Church broke out all over the Christian world.

Amongst the important reformers, next to Luther, who brought about the Reformation came

ULRICH ZWINGLI

Zwingli, the son of Swiss farmers, was given a good education, and as a young man became a chaplain in the army. After years in the army he settled in Zurich where he was offered a pastoral position.

For many political reasons, Switzerland of those days was more advanced in its democratic ideas than most of Europe, and Zwingli was permitted to introduce changes into his church that would not have been tolerated elsewhere.

His first break with the Roman Church came when Zwingli attacked the belief that the priesthood ought never to marry. At the age of forty Zwingli married.

This he followed with an attack on the worship of idols which led to the removal of all pictures, crucifixes and images from all the churches of Zurich.

No sooner was one of his changes successful than Zwingli introduced another.

Zwingli was more advanced in his ideas of Reform than Luther, and on one occasion Luther and Zwingli met in a debate in which the two opposed each other bitterly. In the end Luther was so incensed by Zwingli's ideas that he refused to shake hands with his opponent.

Zwingli hoped to organize the Protestants of Europe and to strengthen them through the support of those rulers who were eager to separate the power of the Church from the power of the State.

Zwingli's hopes were not fulfilled. But in his life and his work he paved the way for another important Reformer:

JOHN CALVIN

The birth of John Calvin in 1509 in Noyon, a little town about seventy miles from Paris, was no great event in the lives of his parents. They had had children before him, and they had children after him.

But when John was old enough to go to school, his

father tried to give his son, together with his other children, the best education to be gotten in their town.

If John's mother was not too busy doing other things, she may have counted the buttons on her second son's shirt, wondering what he would be when he grew up. Preacher? Teacher? Lawyer? Writer? Court Physician? Royal Scribe? Or a Dean in some very great University?

Surely John's mother must have expected him to grow up to be someone very important. For at the age of fourteen John had already exhausted all the learning of Noyon and left for the University of Paris.

After four years in the university John Calvin had distinguished himself for his scholarship. And he kept on studying.

He studied religion. He studied law. He studied Hebrew and Greek. He studied the classics. Five years passed again in studies, and John was still as uncertain as to what career to follow as his mother must have been when she counted the buttons of his shirt. If she did.

Then something happened that decided the question of his career for John Calvin.

A friend of his, a physician, asked him to write an address for him, and John Calvin wrote it. In that address Calvin expressed a number of Protestant doctrines. In those days in France they burned people at the stake for being Protestants, and John Calvin fled from France to Switzerland.

Three years later, when Calvin was still in his twenties, his book, the *Institutes,* appeared. This established him as one of the most important religious writers on Christianity.

From then on Calvin devoted himself to the writing of Protestant works and to the organization of the Protestant Church. He lived almost all his life in Geneva, Switzerland, but his teachings, called *Calvinism,* spread over Europe and took root everywhere.

Calvin personally influenced another noted Church Reformer:

JOHN KNOX

Knox was a Scotchman who preached Protestantism in Scotland and had to flee, for his safety, from his homeland. He went to Geneva, and there he became acquainted with Calvin and his teachings.

When Knox returned to Scotland he established a church very much on the Calvinistic order, excepting for some small differences. His church grew in popularity and his teachings, called *Presbyterianism,* later spread and grew into a large sect.

Presbyterianism played a very important part in the country of its birth, England. But even before John Knox began to preach reform, a great change had taken place in the church of his land which is called

The Church of England

In the British Museum there is a document dating back to 314 A.D. and signed by three British bishops—indicating that Christianity had reached England from Scotland and Ireland very early. But it was not until 597 A.D. that the Pope of Rome sent Augustine to convert the Saxons and to establish the English Branch of the Roman Catholic Church, called the Church of England.

Several hundred years later the English Rulers wished to break the power of the Pope. Unlike the leaders of the Reformation, they had nothing against the *religion* of the Pope, but they did object to his *political* power. And so in 1534 the heads of the Church of England resolved that the Pope of Rome had no greater authority in England than any other foreign Bishop. And from then on the Church of England has been separated from the Roman Catholic Church. (In America the Church of England is known as the *Protestant Episcopal Church.*)

Though the Church of England had broken away from the power of the Pope, its beliefs, ritual and Ministry remained almost the same as those of the Roman Catholic Church.

But the Protestant sects who tried to break away from Catholicism and its teachings, in England as well as in all other parts of the world, kept steadily growing, each one differing from the other in some of their beliefs and practices.

The followers of one of the most important of these sects were known as the

Anabaptists

The Anabaptists appeared soon after the spread of the teachings of Peter Waldo and his followers. By the time

Luther and Zwingli began to organize the Protestant Churches, the Anabaptists were already many in number. Yet, for many reasons, Luther and Zwingli did not find in them friends, particularly because the Anabaptists did not believe in Infant Baptism and Luther and Zwingli did.

It is interesting to us today to read what treatment these Anabaptists received from the hands of the reformers. Between 1517, when Luther first posted his defiance against Indulgences, and 1530, when the teachings of Luther and Zwingli had won over a large following, over 2000 Anabaptists were executed. And the cruelty with which the reformers killed the Anabaptists reminds one of the methods of the Inquisition.

Hounded both by Catholics and Protestants, driven from place to place, killed and imprisoned wherever found, yet their numbers swelled and their teachings spread in Switzerland, Germany, Austria and Holland.

The Anabaptists were the forerunners of a number of important Protestant sects, amongst them the *Baptists* of today, the *Congregationalists,* and

THE QUAKERS

The Quakers, who arose in England towards the end of the 17th Century, were unlike any other Christian sect in that they had no definite set of beliefs for their members to profess.

They also had no clergy and no churches.

They believed that the true religion, which they called the Inward Light, was within the individual and that wherever true believers meet, that spot is sacred ground. They met in private homes. They met in barns. They met in the open air and in market-places.

And their meetings were more like a gathering of a group of friends, a Society of Friends.

In fact, that is what they really called themselves: *The Society of Friends*.

("Quakers" is only a nickname that clung to them, just as the nickname "Methodists" clung to another Christian sect.)

The Quakers were persecuted in England, and many of them migrated to America. But they received no better treatment here, until one Quaker, William Penn, started a Quaker colony in what is now Pennsylvania and New Jersey.

The Quakers were influenced by the teachings of other sects that came before them. And they, in turn, influenced sects that came after them.

And the multiplication of the Protestant sects continued.

Some of these sects are so different from one another that they almost do not seem branches of the same religion. Others are so much alike that it might be wondered why they are not united in one sect and one church. Some have Founders of their own whom they call Saints and Prophets. Some have Sacred Scriptures of their own besides the Bible. And some have ways of worship not shared by any of the others.

The division of the Protestant sects has gone on since the Reformation, until, today, there are about two hundred and fify different sects, and new sects still continue to appear.

7. THE AMERICAN-BORN SECTS

In America every type of Christian is to be found. Greek Orthodox, Roman Catholic, and almost all of the two hundred different Protestant sects are represented here.

In addition to the European-born Christian sects that thrive in America, we have a number that originated on American soil.

The most outstanding of the American sects are: *Mormonism,* and *Christian Science.*

Mormonism was established about a century ago by Joseph Smith, of the State of New York, who claimed to have found a book written on golden plates, revealed to him by an angel called Moroni. Joseph Smith with some friends organized a new church, which they called:

The Church of Jesus of Latter-day Saints.

The members of this church are called *Mormons,* believers in *The Book of Mormon* found by Joseph Smith.

There are about half a million Mormons in the world today, most of them in or around Salt Lake City, Utah. Yet they firmly believe and proclaim to the world that theirs is:

"The only true and living church upon the face of the whole earth."

Much more recent in appearance is the sect known as *Christian Science,* founded in 1879 by a New England woman, Mrs. Mary Baker Eddy.

Mrs. Eddy wrote a book, called: *Science and Health: With a Key to the Scriptures,* in which she tried to explain how the sick can be healed through faith.

Mrs. Eddy, like Joseph Smith and many others before her, organized a church. This church she called:

The First Church of Christ, Scientist.

Mrs. Eddy's church soon found many followers in America as well as in other countries.

Like Mormonism, and like all the sects that appear, Christian Science claims to be the only true Christian Church.

But no matter how the many Protestant sects differ from one another, they all agree:

That one can be a good Christian without paying homage to the Pope; and that

The Roman Catholic Church is not the only true Christian Church in the world.

In Our Own Time

In *the Beginning,* as we have seen, people observed the sun rise and set each day; they heard the wind go through the woods; and saw the clouds gather in the sky. And in time they observed season follow season as night follows day and day follows night.

Man of long ago asked questions about all the forces of nature which surrounded him. And he answered these questions, saying, the Forces of Nature have Spirits that can do both good and evil.

Our savage forefathers, many thousands of years ago, did not know the difference between animate and inanimate things. To them the trees, the flowers, the rivers, the ocean, the stones and the mountains were all alive. They had spirits.

The elements, too, were believed to have spirits.

The sun and the moon and the stars; the rain and the wind and the storm, thunder and lightning—all these were *beings* to our primitive ancestors, beings alive and free to do as they pleased, both good and evil.

This belief in the Spirits of Nature was the beginning of the earliest religion of Mankind. And it led people to worship nature, and animals, and their ancestors.

After many, many years, perhaps centuries, our forefathers passed from Nature Worship to Idol Worship.

Though most people today hold Idolatry (Idol Worship) in contempt, it really marked a great advance over the earlier Nature Worship.

But with the development of Idolatry, the number of things and beings worshipped multiplied rapidly. Images were made not only for all the existing nature-gods, ancestors, and various animals, but also for newly conceived gods, such as the gods of the various families, gods of tribes, gods presiding over the boundary lines between farms, and so on.

And, as we have seen, with the multiplication of the gods came a multiplication of hatred and struggle between tribes and families and individuals.

In time wise leaders realized that at the root of all this evil was Idol Worship and they began to preach against it. And the great religions, as we know them today, came into existence.

Then the belief in many gods gave way to the belief in One God.

This was the greatest advance in the development of religion.

For the belief in One God leads to the belief in the Unity of the World. And this, in turn, leads to the belief in the Unity of Mankind.

The believer in One God (or Monotheist as he is called) realizes that all of mankind must be regarded as one large family, different as may be the color of people's skins, the words of their speech, or the manner of their daily lives.

More than that:

The true Monotheist realizes that whatever any one race does affects all other races; whatever one nation does affects all other nations; whatever one person does affects all other people—for good or for evil.

And from this the true Monotheist is forced to conclude that only what is good for mankind at large is good for the individual. And what is bad for mankind is bad for the individual in the long run.

This is what is meant by the Brotherhood of Man that all the great religions of today preach.

And this Brotherhood of Man can be attained not through hatred, but love; not through strife, but cooperation; not through war, but peace.

So that in our own time, in a world full of pain and confusion and bitterness, the world's religions find themselves faced with one great common mission:

The Mission of Peace.

Regardless of the differences between religion and religion, or creed and creed, to fulfill their promise to their followers, they must all gather under the one banner bearing the inscription:

The Mission of Mankind is Peace.

INDEX

The MENTOR Religious Classics

☐ **THE MEANING OF THE GLORIOUS KORAN: An Explanatory Translation by Mohammed Marmaduke Pickthall.** The complete sacred book of Mohammedanism, translated with reverence and scholarship.
(#MW1195—$1.50)

☐ **HERE I STAND: A LIFE OF MARTIN LUTHER by Roland H. Bainton.** A vivid portrait of the man whose unshakeable faith in his God helped to establish Protestantism.
(#MY1133—$1.25)

☐ **THE SONG OF GOD: BHAGAVAD-GITA translated by Swami Prabhavananda and Christopher Isherwood.** A distinguished translation of the Gospel of Hinduism, one of the great religious classics of the world. Introduction by Aldous Huxley. Appendices. (#MQ1003—95¢)

☐ **THE UPANISHADS: BREATH OF THE ETERNAL translated by Swami Prabhavananda and Frederick Manchester.** Here is the wisdom of the Hindu mystics in principal texts selected and translated from the original Sanskrit.
(#MQ921—95¢)

☐ **THE LIVING TALMUD: THE WISDOM OF THE FATHERS AND ITS CLASSICAL COMMENTARIES selected and translated by Judah Goldin.** A new translation, with an illuminating essay on the place of the Talmud in Jewish life and religion. (#MQ1024—95¢)

☐ **ISLAM IN MODERN HISTORY by Wilfred Cantwell Smith.** A discussion of the impact of Mohammedanism on the political life of the Middle East today.
(#MY1108—$1.25)

THE NEW AMERICAN LIBRARY, INC.,
P.O. Box 999, Bergenfield, New Jersey 07621

Please send me the MENTOR BOOKS I have checked above. I am enclosing $_____(check or money order—no currency or C.O.D.'s). Please include the list price plus 15¢ a copy to cover handling and mailing costs. (Prices and numbers are subject to change without notice.)

Name_____

Address_____

City_____State_____Zip Code_____

Allow at least 3 weeks for delivery

SIGNET and MENTOR Books of Special Interest

☐ **THE STORY BIBLE: Volume I by Pearl S. Buck.** The winner of the Nobel and Pulitzer Prizes retells the Greatest Story Ever Told in the living language of our times. In VOLUME I, the immortal stories of the Old Testament are brought to life with a power and immediacy for the modern reader. (#Y5080—$1.25)

☐ **THE STORY BIBLE: VOLUME II by Pearl S. Buck.** This superlative rendering of the New Testament brings the crowning achievement of Pearl Buck's career, THE STORY BIBLE, to a triumphant conclusion. Here, adding relevance to its wisdom and freshness to its beauty, is the story of the birth, life, death and resurrection of Jesus. "Compelling, moving . . ."—**Library Journal** (#Y5079—$1.25)

☐ **PSYCHOANALYSIS AND PERSONALITY by Joseph Nuttin.** The noted Belgian psychologist discusses the relation between modern depth psychology and Christian philosophy. (#MY950—$1.25)

☐ **LEISURE: THE BASIS OF CULTURE by Josef Pieper.** A series of essays indicting the 20th century interpretation of leisure as a time for hectic amusement, and warning that unless we regain the art of silence and insight, we will ultimately destroy our culture—and ourselves. Introduction by T. S. Eliot. (#MQ1048—95¢)

☐ **MARIA MONTESSORI: HER LIFE AND WORK by E. M. Standing.** A biography of the great educator by a friend and colleague, who evaluates her contributions to contemporary education. Eight pages of photographs. (#MW1009—$1.50)

THE NEW AMERICAN LIBRARY, INC.,
P.O. Box 999, Bergenfield, New Jersey 07621

Please send me the SIGNET and MENTOR BOOKS I have checked above. I am enclosing $_____(check or money order—no currency or C.O.D.'s). Please include the list price plus 15¢ a copy to cover handling and mailing costs. (Prices and numbers are subject to change without notice.)

Name_____

Address_____

City_____State_____Zip Code_____
Allow at least 3 weeks for delivery

The MENTOR Philosophers

The entire range of Western speculative thinking from the Middle Ages to modern times is presented in this series of six volumes. Each book contains the basic writings of the leading philosophers of each age, with introduction and commentary by noted authorities.

"A very important and interesting series."

—Gilbert Highet

☐ **THE AGE OF BELIEF: THE MEDIEVAL PHILOSOPHERS edited by Anne Fremantle.** "Highly commendable . . . provides an excellent beginning volume."—**The Classical Bulletin** (#MY1020—$1.25)

☐ **THE AGE OF ADVENTURE: THE RENAISSANCE PHILOSOPHERS edited by Georgio de Santillana.** "The most exciting and varied in the series."—**New York Times** (#MQ835—95¢)

☐ **THE AGE OF REASON: THE 17TH CENTURY PHILOSOPHERS edited by Stuart Hampshire.** "His (Hampshire's) book is a most satisfactory addition to an excellent series."—**Saturday Review** (#MY1186—$1.25)

☐ **THE AGE OF ENLIGHTENMENT: THE 18TH CENTURY PHILOSOPHERS edited by Sir Isaiah Berlin.** "(Sir Isaiah) has one of the liveliest and most stimulating minds among contemporary philosophers."—**New York Herald Tribune** (#MY1213—$1.25)

☐ **THE AGE OF IDEOLOGY: THE 19TH CENTURY PHILOSOPHERS edited by Henry D. Aiken.** ". . . perhaps the most distinct intellectual contribution made in the series."—**New York Times** (#MY1019—$1.25)

☐ **THE AGE OF ANALYSIS: 20TH CENTURY PHILOSOPHERS edited by Morton White.** "No other book remotely rivals this as the best available introduction to 20th century philosophy."—**N. Y. Herald Tribune** (#MW1179—$1.50)

THE NEW AMERICAN LIBRARY, INC.,
P.O. Box 999, Bergenfield, New Jersey 07621

Please send me the MENTOR BOOKS I have checked above. I am enclosing $_____(check or money order—no currency or C.O.D.'s). Please include the list price plus 15¢ a copy to cover handling and mailing costs. (Prices and numbers are subject to change without notice.)

Name_____

Address_____

City_____State_____Zip Code_____

Allow at least 3 weeks for delivery